SAVE OUR SPECIES

ALSO BY THE AUTHOR

SAVE OUR SPECIES

Endangered Animals and How You Can Save Them

DOMINIC COUZENS

ILLUSTRATIONS BY SARAH EDMONDS

HarperCollins*Publishers*

HarperCollins*Publishers*
1 London Bridge Street
London SE1 9GF

www.harpercollins.co.uk

HarperCollins*Publishers*
1st Floor, Watermarque Building, Ringsend Road
Dublin 4, Ireland

First published by HarperCollins*Publishers* 2021

1 3 5 7 9 10 8 6 4 2

A catalogue record of this book is available from the British Library

ISBN 978-0-00-843861-6

Printed and bound in Great Britain by CPI Group (UK) Ltd, Croydon

Contents

Introduction

Britain's nature is in serious trouble. Thanks for being part of the solution. You care about nature, and that is incredibly important. Our wildlife needs you on board desperately. With enough people on its side, nature in this country has a chance to thrive again.

Nature can be resurgent if we let it happen. It requires political will and action but, more than anything, nature needs advocates, people who care about the issues and want solutions. Nature needs serious, knowledgeable people who know that they will lose some battles but can also gain ground. The UK will never return to its primal state, full of vast tracts of unsettled wilderness and hardly any people. But some areas can be rewilded; it even makes economic sense to do so. And a great deal can be done to ameliorate the destruction of our wildlife, which, particularly since the 1950s and 1960s, has been horrendous.

This book is designed to play a role, however small, in that process. It contains the stories of 30 animals and plants that have declined in our country, setting out the reasons why they are in trouble. But it also makes suggestions as to how we can help the species.

It also presents ideas about how you and I can help wildlife in general, starting now. A lot of these, surprisingly but encouragingly, start in gardens and neighbourhoods. Many people don't realise how important their personal contributions are. They are important because they signify a person won over. If enough people are won over, and convinced that their voice can be heard, conservation can still do great things.

First, though, we need to get an idea of the problems.

Our country's biodiversity is falling rapidly, by almost every measure. Each year, a partnership of more than 50 conservation and research organisations brings out a report called *State of Nature*, and the most recent version makes typically grim reading:

- The total number of breeding birds in the UK fell by 44 million between 1967 and 2009.
- The abundance of butterflies in Britain has shrunk by 16% since 1976 and the abundance of moths has fallen by 25% since 1970.
- A sample of 696 typical terrestrial and freshwater species of all kinds shows a decline in average abundance of 13% since 1970; even more alarmingly, the same sample shows a 6% decline in the last ten years alone.
- A measure of species for which there are reliable population criteria, totalling 8,431 in all, suggests that, of these, 1,188 (15%) are threatened with extinction from Great Britain, while 2% have gone already.

Within these complex figures are many individual stories. For example, skylarks have declined by over 75% since the 1950s and hedgehogs could be down 90%. Some species have increased, of course, such as red kites, bitterns and pine martens. But what really stands out is the number of familiar species that have suddenly dropped and are in danger of becoming history. This is where the damage to our wildlife becomes personal. Those of us who love listening to the glorious songs of skylarks and the chirping of sparrows cannot bear to think that their world and ours is now so diminished.

There is barely a corner of Britain, or a type of habitat, excluded from the grim tally. In Britain, all manner of wildlife-rich habitats have been lost to development, not just recently but for centuries. Chalk downlands, heaths, bogs, freshwater marshes, seacoasts, estuaries, Caledonian pine forests and meadows are all examples of habitats that have shrunk vastly in area as human reach and exploitation has expanded. We have, for example, lost 97% of our flower-rich meadows since the 1930s.

It could be suggested that development for housing and industry was the biggest driver of destruction up to the war years. But since then, a newer crisis has emerged on Britain's farmland, which covers 70% of our surface area. Farmland was once a good habitat for many birds, invertebrates, flowers and much else, animals and plants benefiting from a share of production and space. But spurred by the need to produce more food, farms became much more efficient and intensive. Hedgerows were grubbed up (c.50% of pre-war levels remains), ponds drained, corners evened out, stubbles removed. The soil was subjected to a barrage of chemicals, and still is. There was a wide switch from spring to autumn sowing. Everything became cleaner and more efficient, but at a terrible cost to biodiversity.

At the same time, there has been industrial-scale persecution of wildlife. Predators were culled in enormous numbers, fish stocks were depleted, and animals and plants abused. Gardening followed farming into a weird type of intensification, with tidiness in vogue and perfection a sort of creed. Other ills the environment suffered included pollution, changes in hydrology, the introduction of harmful non-native species and, more recently, the creep of climate change.

These changes did not go unnoticed. Many people began to realise that Britain's biodiversity was collapsing. But the political will was slow to accept that change was needed in the rate of 'progress'.

It still is. Governments of the day kick environmental concerns into the long grass. Decision makers are in thrall to the lobbyists for big business, and economics seems to be entranced by models – such as 'growth' – which mean very little and pay no attention to quality of life. So rapacious developers are allowed still to look upon natural places and salivate. Farming is still trapped in its intensive model, even when in some cases it would make more economic and environmental sense to change tack. Big infrastructure projects still make politicians' eyes light up. We are caught in a cultural insanity that holds tidiness in high esteem in the garden, yet leaves the countryside littered. We are on planet Earth, which is warming rapidly, with alarming consequences that most of us hardly dare to think about and some deny. Nobody can truly be sure what medicine climate change will force us to take, although the most authoritative voices are frightening.

Despite this, though, there is room for optimism. Conservationists have tended to be caught in a spiral of despair in recent years. To get a flavour, all you need to do is tap into some of the conservation threads on Twitter. But it doesn't need to be like this. We have perhaps swallowed the misconception that environmental solutions are too difficult and too slow to implement and the economy always wins, because that is our experience. This needn't be true at all. Nobody pretends that it is easy to save Britain's wildlife; what we mustn't conclude is that it is impossible to make enormous progress.

A question worth asking at this point is: do we actually need to save our country's natural heritage? If we let things go on as they are now, what might happen? After all, Britain is a severely degraded country. In world terms, it doesn't stand out in terms of resources or biodiversity. Can we just get on with our lives and not worry?

There are many reasons why we need to do something, but three are perhaps especially important. The first is that wild animals and plants share our Earth; don't we have a moral right to look after them as well as ourselves? Secondly, if we damage the environment, we might damage ourselves. Already we know that pollution is harmful, affecting what we drink and what we breathe. The fate of other animals is intertwined with ours. The farming environment is awash with chemicals to kill plants and invertebrates. If these are damaging biodiversity, then surely they will damage us, too. Looking after the natural world is a deterrent against self-harm.

And thirdly, we now know that nature is a great tonic for our well-being. Study after study in the scientific and medical sphere suggests that exposure to wild places is good for us, makes us happier and fights against mental health issues, such as depression and stress. Even in the city, people need access to green spaces, and the country as a whole needs room to breathe. If there was no other reason to look after the natural world, this one is surely decisive on its own?

There is an oft-quoted statistic about the membership of the Royal Society for the Protection of Birds (RSPB). This organisation currently has a membership of about a million, which is as much as the Conservative, Labour, Liberal Democratic and Scottish National Parties combined. This is a force that politicians should ignore at their peril.

But they always seem to have other priorities. The disconnect is echoed in the figures quoted in the most recent *State of Nature* report. Public support for conservation is on the increase. People are giving more money and more time. The various conservation organisations spent 26% more between 2010/11 and 2018/19, reflecting their income. Meanwhile, there was a huge increase in the amount of time given up by volunteers – up 46% since 2000.

At the same time, government expenditure on biodiversity in this country is miserly. As a proportion of gross domestic product (GDP), it has actually fallen by 42% since 2008/09. This is unabashed failure. This frankly pathetic lack of political will is far more dangerous than it sounds. As the climate crisis rages, interest and commitment to conservation is growing, and more and more people are finding refuge in nature, our government's commitment to biodiversity is falling. If ever there was proof that the ruling class doesn't 'get it', perhaps those bald figures spell it out.

The former Conservative Party leader William Hague recently said: '… no one should think that our own age will in future be regarded as the highest point of human morality. I am convinced that generations to come will regard our abuse and degradation of the natural world as little short of barbarism.' It is hard not to agree. It is a hopeful sign that he and many others in the corridors of power are waking up. Is it not possible that in our lifetime, the environment can roar on to the public's agenda and become a concern that strikes at the heart of every politician's soft spot – their electoral potential? Then perhaps the time-honoured slogan will need to be modified to: 'It's the environment, stupid.'

We may not be far from the natural world becoming an urgent political imperative. We might be approaching a tipping point at which government is simply forced to look after wildlife. If this is to be realised, though, those in power need to be convinced that enough people care.

There are many inspiring stories in this book that tell of heroic steps to save species. People fought to ensure that seahorses were legally protected, others reintroduced the large blue butterfly, still others are battling at great personal cost to fight against the illegal killing of raptors on grouse moors. Many farmers are bravely going organic or deciding to fit biodiversity into their management schemes. People are fighting to keep rivers clean and others wake up early in the morning to clear up litter from the night before. There are scientists, teachers and social media warriors holding power to account. It is truly humbling to see what has already been achieved. The scientists even know how to save the skylark.

Now, perhaps, it is about troops on the ground. We stand at a crossroads. With enough public support, we can win many conservation battles. We can help make the world a better place, with room for nature. If we reach a critical mass of public opinion, and people being concerned, we might reach a tipping point that makes the successes detailed above become more and more frequent.

We need everybody. We need Generation Z and the millennials to come to our aid, fresh from their activism for social rights, now to be engaged in another fight for justice.

We need people who love their gardens. We need people who love watching wildlife on the telly. We need people from our urban centres to come to see how amazing nature is, and to be made welcome.

Everybody's small steps, as detailed here in many sections on ways you can help, add up to an exciting journey towards a richer country at environmental ease with itself. We might win the fight for Britain's wildlife. Let's see.

FACT FILES

The fact files for each species contain a summary of information about its conservation. These include its status and its chances of surviving in Britain to 2050. These are explained below.

STATUS

All plants and animals are placed in so-called Red List categories by the International Union for the Conservation of Nature (IUCN) describing their conservation prospects, either on a worldwide scale, a regional scale (e.g. Europe) or in the countries where they occur. A complicated and statistical evaluation of an animal or plant's prospects is determined by such things as their overall range, overall population and how that range or population might have reduced. The categories are as follows:

- Critically Endangered – extremely high risk of extinction in the wild.
- Endangered – very high risk of extinction in the wild.
- Vulnerable – high risk of extinction in the wild.
- Near Threatened – does not yet meet any criteria for the above categories but is close at the moment and might be upgraded in the near future.
- Least Concern – does not qualify for any of the above categories.

In addition, the RSPB classifies birds into three lists of Conservation Concern:

- Red List – the species is either globally threatened, there has been a historical decline between 1800 and 1995, or there has been a 50% or more reduction in breeding range or population over the last 25 years (or since 1969).
- Amber List – this species may have unfavourable conservation status in Europe; it might have declined between 1800 and1995 but be recovering; suffering a 25–50% decline in UK breeding range or population; a non-breeding bird suffering a 25–50% decline; a naturally rare bird; or Britain may account for 20% or more of its breeding or non-breeding population.
- Green List – none of the above.

Finally, some animals and plants are part of the UK's Biodiversity Action Plans. They are subject to government plans for priority species and habitats in the UK that are most under threat. The plans are intended to aid their recovery.

CHANCES OF SURVIVING IN BRITAIN TO 2050

These are the author's best guesses for an animal or plant's chances (out of five):

1 It has only a small chance of surviving here to 2050; hanging by a thread.
2 In great trouble, but conservation efforts are giving it a chance.
3 In trouble, but actual extinction is unlikely.
4 Problems are great but animal or plant is resilient.
5 Unlikely to disappear without complete catastrophe, but still declining badly.

Hedgehog

Erinaceus europaeus

FACT FILE

DISTRIBUTION

Widespread throughout most of the UK.

CURRENT STATUS

Vulnerable.

PAST AND CURRENT POPULATIONS

Approximately 30 million in the 1950s. Currently estimated at 522,000. We have lost 30% of our population since 2002.

DESCRIPTION OF THE SPECIES

22–27cm long. Britain's only spiny mammal, with 5,000 modified hairs on its back, so unmistakable. Small eyes and ears and button nose. Has shuffling gait. Hibernates from November to March.

DESCRIPTION OF THE THREATS

Agricultural intensification has reduced the quality of its habitat. Pesticide use and incompatible garden designs (e.g. fewer lawns); roadkill; predation by record high number of badgers.

WHAT WE NEED TO DO

Adapt our gardens to suit hedgehogs, so don't use slug pellets and other pesticides; allow untidiness; build runways between gardens.

ORGANISATIONS TO SUPPORT

British Hedgehog Preservation Society; People's Trust for Endangered Species (PTES).

CHANCES OF SURVIVAL IN BRITAIN TO 2050

5/5

Remember the old days when we used to worry about tigers and giant pandas disappearing? Back then, not really long ago, the idea that we might lose common animals such as hedgehogs would never have entered our minds. Here we are, though. There were once millions of hedgehogs in Britain; nobody bothered to count them because there were so many. They found their way into Britons' hearts, partly through the highly effective medium of children's books (remember Mrs Tiggywinkle?), and partly because they would share our lawns, even if we lived in towns and cities. Householders used to put out bread and milk for their local hog (a practice now strongly discouraged because it can upset their tummies). They were part of the twilight British summer. In the 1950s there may have been 30 million hedgehogs in Britain.

Where are we now? People began to notice a decline from the 1960s onwards. Later on, this became measurable, ironically through the medium of finding fewer squashed road casualties, which diminished by 20–30% through the 1990s. By the 2000s there were still thought to be 1.5 million hedgehogs in Britain. However, since then their fall in numbers has begun to accelerate, possibly by as much as 73% since 1995. The current estimate of 500,000 or so could conceivably add up to only 2% of what it used to be. Although the hedgehog is relatively common in places, its overall situation has led to it being classified as Vulnerable (just one step back from Endangered). It is unlikely to disappear completely but could become so uncommon as to be eroded from our national consciousness.

In many ways, the hedgehog has become like the house sparrow, a backyard staple that has become suddenly precious. How did it come to this? And is there anything we can do about it?

The plight of the hedgehog is complicated. There is no doubt that the perfect storm of agricultural intensification – fewer hedgerows; fewer untidy, unprofitable corners; more poisonous pesticides and herbicides – has dramatically impacted on hedgehogs, as it has on so many species. Another problem is the hedgehog's unfortunate relationship with car tyres; the hedgehog prospered in a slower, less busy world. One estimate puts the annual hedgehog road mortality at 167,000–350,000. There is little we can do about this. Imagine trying to ask car drivers to slow down? Yeah, right.

Hedgehogs also have a troubling relationship with badgers. Well, it is troubling for the hedgehogs, because badgers eat them. The claws of the larger animal are powerful and sharp enough to breach those spiny defences. Not long ago, when hedgehogs were common and badgers scarcer than they are today, this was merely unfortunate for the predated hog. But badger numbers are thought to have doubled since the 1980s, and studies show that, where badgers are densely populated, hedgehogs disappear. Badger numbers are at a historic high and are even finding their way into the urban fringe, a traditional safe zone for hogs.

However, it isn't all bad news because, as we know, hedgehogs can still thrive in gardens, in towns and cities. And here we can make a difference, because we can make our own patch of land – or nearby shared spaces – hedgehog-friendly.

But in order to help hedgehogs, we need to break some habits. Hogs are carnivorous, eating a wide range of animal matter, mainly invertebrates. Worms and beetle larvae are firm favourites. Good food needs good habitat, which means, for a start, keep your lawn intact. Unless you have mobility issues, decking isn't favourable and, in particular, do everything you can to avoid that modern-day monstrosity, the plastic lawn. Put your plastic lawn provider out of business, please. Secondly, stop all use of slug pellets and other pesticides, and make your garden free of chemicals. If you can bear to, allow some patches of long grass and general untidiness: this is where the hedgehog's food thrives.

The hedgehog is admirable, but for an animal that has survived for millions of years, it is remarkably accident prone – but then again, maybe modern human weirdness is the accident. We like to put netting over our vegetables, but if we allow the netting down to the ground the hedgehogs' spines can become trapped. Hogs can also get caught up in various types of litter. If we have a pond that is steep-sided, they may fall in and drown.

If we mow or, in particular, strim the lawn, we need to be careful not to kill a hedgehog in the process. These animals sometimes lie up in long grass during the day. The widespread and expensive practice of strimming roadsides and amenity sites can also kill hedgehogs, but nobody knows how much destruction this wreaks. Much council strimming is no more than a sop to stridently noisy individuals who complain about 'untidiness'. Such attitudes should be resisted. Who really wants perfectly manicured, sterile streets and parks anyway? It's probably a minority. Some verge-strimming is necessary for safety reasons, but much is not.

Similarly, hedgehogs are drawn to piles of vegetation, so bonfires, especially those lit in celebration of Guy Fawkes Night, 5 November, should carefully be checked for hedgehogs before they are lit. Hedgehogs often hibernate early in such attractive looking habitats, so they are particularly vulnerable in their sleepy state.

Apart from resisting temptations to be over-tidy and zealous, there are also more positive ways to help the hogs. Modern gardens are often enclosed by high walls and fences, so if you can make sure that there are gaps or passageways (13cm by 13cm) in your boundaries, you will allow hedgehogs access to a wide foraging area – creating so-called 'Hedgehog Highways'. You can also become a Hedgehog Champion, make your street a Hedgehog Street and your town – guess what? – a Hedgehog Town, all by increasing local awareness. The People's Trust for Endangered Species runs all these initiatives and would value any time or financial support you are able to give.

If you are lucky enough to have hogs grace your garden, you can effectively become their host. Put out a hedgehog box (see page 190 for full instructions), especially if you wish to encourage them to hibernate or even raise a litter. And, of course, you can provide them with meals. Shun the bread and milk, but give them meaty cat or dog food, or even cat biscuits. The garden centre will no doubt stock some expensive hedgehog mix, too. And don't forget to put out the odd dish of water on warm nights.

The future of British hedgehogs almost certainly lies in the hands of gardeners and those who look after open spaces.

Grey Long-eared Bat

Plecotus austriacus

--- **FACT FILE** ---

DISTRIBUTION

South coast of England, including the Isle of Wight.

CURRENT ENDANGERED STATUS

Endangered.

PAST AND CURRENT POPULATIONS

Past unknown. Current 1,000.

DESCRIPTION OF THE SPECIES

Wingspan 25—30cm, length 4—6cm. A medium-sized bat with exceptionally long ears that dominate its profile. Ears are forward-facing and meet on forehead. Almost identical to another species, brown long-eared bat.

DESCRIPTION OF THE THREATS

Loss of wetlands and species-rich meadows for foraging; encroachment of urban development; rural building conversions; light pollution; traffic collisions.

WHAT WE NEED TO DO

Keep the known colonies and their buildings intact. Help bats generally with less artificial light; grow lots of night-scented flowers; drive more carefully.

ORGANISATIONS TO SUPPORT

Bat Conservation Trust.

CHANCES OF SURVIVAL IN BRITAIN TO 2050

2/5

You think nightlife in the countryside is boring? Just ask a bat. Bats are among our most remarkable creatures. A small bat can eat 1,000 midges a night. Bats can fly through the branches of a tree or pluck a tiny fish from the water surface without looking. Some can hear partly using their noses. They sometimes feed on the ground. Several species gather in mating swarms in autumn. They give birth while hanging upside down. They sleep for most of the winter, but males sometimes impregnate hibernating females. A small bat can fit into a large matchbox but live for 30 years. Their heartbeat rate is ten times that of ours. Meanwhile, we sometimes have trouble telling bat species apart without looking at their penises.

Bats are extraordinary, indeed. Many people are frightened of them. This could partly be because they are other-worldly and nocturnal but is perhaps as much related to their bad press. If a moviemaker wishes to set a scene to evoke a dash of menace, it seems they just add darkness, a churchyard and a bat. The novel *Dracula* hardly helped. Neither does the fact that vampire bats do exist, do drink blood and will bite humans and also spread some diseases. British bats, on the other hand, don't drink blood, they won't fly into your hair, and actually eat mosquitos – which do both!

You might feel vulnerable when bats flit over your head, but the real peril isn't yours. Bats should fear us. After all, we have persecuted them for centuries out of fear and superstition, and in the modern world they face a formidable tranche of difficulties and hazards which are caused by humankind. The list of threats to bats is long and varied, partly to do with bats' complicated lifestyle: they need a site to breed, a site to spend the summer if not breeding and a site to hibernate which needs to be just right for them.

They feed on flying insects, and so they are highly vulnerable to insect populations, and also the weather.

So, just look at all these issues. Bats are threatened by development encroaching into the countryside; by a large downturn in the populations of their main food, moths; by being struck by wind turbines; by being struck by cars; by the development of large rural buildings; by being caught by cats; by changes in woodland management, allowing for fewer old and rotten trees; by the loss of meadows and other prime habitats; by light pollution. With so much going badly for them in the larger environment, it's a wonder we have any bats left at all.

In the case of the grey long-eared bat, its continued existence in Britain is precarious. There are only ten breeding sites (maternity roosts) known, while its hibernation sites have not yet been discovered. All the maternity roosts are in the lofts of large buildings in small villages along the coast of southern England, each of them a Victorian house with roomy access to the loft (for a bat). The precarious population of 1,000 or so individuals comes out late at night to feed on moths, especially in deep countryside. They fly slowly, and often low down, so are sometimes hit by cars. Their most pressing threat is the loss of traditional meadows and wet pastureland, which often gives way to more intensive farming.

Britain's 17 bat species are well protected by law. As many landowners know only too well, the presence of bats can put a hold on buidling developments, which can understandably be annoying. It is illegal to disturb a bat roost intentionally, to kill or to injure a bat or to prevent bats' access to a roost. The law demands surveys and mitigation, which can be expensive. However, what is the alternative? Do we want fewer animals sharing our space?

These days, people's attitudes towards bats are changing for the better, especially among the young. Thankfully, more and more people are finding bats to be the remarkable and admirable animals they are. There is much still to be done, though, to educate people.

Wherever you are reading this book, you will be close to a place where bats live, and you can make a difference in helping them. The first step is to become a bat enthusiast yourself. If you do, perhaps you can point out bats to your friends and neighbours, or even lead a local walk pointing them out. You can buy a bat detector, which turns the bats' ultrasonic clicks into entertaining clicks and flatulent sounds and helps you identify the species. These things make a big difference in communities. If you become competent in bat detecting, which is not difficult, you could get involved with the National Bat Monitoring Scheme.

The second thing you can do is to make space for bats yourself. The obvious way is to put up a bat box in a garden, a school building or in public land. Bat boxes are relatively inexpensive, or you can even make one (see page 189). They look like bird boxes, but the entrance is a slit in the bottom.

Another way to improve your local area for bats is to plant night-scented flowers, which attract the moths that the bats eat (see page 141). A garden pond is also a great idea, because this also attracts flying insects. If you are ambitious and forward thinking, you could arrange to plant a linear feature such as a hedgerow or row of trees. There is some excellent advice on what to plant on the Royal Horticultural Society (RHS) website. Also, the Tree Council website provides all kinds of helpful advice. If at all possible, reducing artificial lighting is also very helpful for bats (see page 218).

We are fortunate that bats share our communities with us. Many roost and breed in houses and other buildings, such as churches. In contrast to some animals, which need expensive conservation measures, we can all help bats relatively easily – as easily, indeed, as the birds in our parks and gardens.

Red Squirrel

Sciurus vulgaris

FACT FILE

DISTRIBUTION

Forests and woods in Scotland, northern England, Northern Ireland. Hanging on in Wales. Also islands such as Anglesey and Isle of Wight.

CURRENT STATUS

Endangered (England and Wales); Near Threatened (Scotland).

PAST AND CURRENT POPULATIONS

Current 287,000. Past unknown, but probably in the millions.

DESCRIPTION OF THE SPECIES

18–24cm long, plus tail 14–20cm. Smaller than grey squirrel, with smart chestnut fur contrasting with white belly, distinctive ear-tufts. Tail may bleach whitish in summer.

DESCRIPTION OF THE THREATS

Infectious diseases such as Squirrel Pox Virus, spread by grey squirrels; competition for food and resources with greys; forestry practice, especially growing of Sitka spruce, which red squirrels don't like.

WHAT WE NEED TO DO

Local trapping of grey squirrels; artificial feeding to allow public to see red squirrels; ensure that bird feeders in gardens don't make life too easy for grey squirrels; reintroduce pine martens in some areas.

ORGANISATIONS TO SUPPORT

Red Squirrels United; Mammal Society.

CHANCES OF SURVIVAL IN BRITAIN TO 2050

4/5

To its legion of admirers, the red squirrel is one of Britain's most attractive animals. It isn't difficult to share the view; the animal is simply gorgeous. You can almost imagine its nemesis, the grey squirrel, looking enviously at it and thinking: 'Lose weight, grow funky ear tufts, dye my fur, take more exercise ...'

Through the eyes of certain of our forebears, however, the red squirrel was not attractive enough. It was so familiar as to be viewed with condescension. There was a prevailing feeling in Victorian times that you could improve the British landscape by introducing novel animals, and in 1876 they introduced the grey squirrel, from North America. This was neither an accident, nor was it a one-off. From late Victorian times people kept on replenishing stocks of grey squirrels, even as recently as 1930, including 100 animals into Richmond Park, in Greater London, in 1902. It was introduced to Ireland in 1911. It has, though, proven to be one of Britain's most famous ecological self-inflicted wounds.

We cannot know how many red squirrels there were around 1876, but it would number in the millions. It was common in many parts of the British Isles, in all kinds of woodlands. It had always been subject to wildly fluctuating fortunes on our islands, partly as a result of deforestation and hunting, and partly owing to its vulnerability to squirrelpox virus (SQPV). Nevertheless, it was common and widespread until at least 1940. Ever since then it has begun to decline and, even today, it is still in retreat. From inhabiting the whole country, it has shrunk in range to parts of Scotland, northern England, Northern Ireland, remote Wales and a few islands, including Anglesey and the Isle of Wight. At the same time, the grey squirrel has gone from zero to about 2.7 million, taking over where the red squirrel once thrived.

It is easy to see the grey rise and the red sunset as a binary story of good and bad, but the relationship between the two closely related animals is much subtler than that. Grey squirrels don't directly kill reds, and in some places the two species have been known to live close by each other for as long as 20 years. In some woodlands, though, the newcomers have a habit of pilfering the seed caches of red squirrels in the springtime, causing the reds to enter the breeding season with lower body mass, a sign of poor condition and resulting in lower productivity. Red squirrels simply don't thrive in the presence of greys. However, the biggest difference between the two is that grey squirrels are immune to SQPV. If there is an outbreak, which could be spread by grey squirrels, it is the reds that succumb. Outbreaks of this disease firmly and permanently tip the scales in favour of the newcomers.

Of course, back in Victorian times, they didn't mean to cause any harm and might well have been appalled had they known what a disaster they had unleased. And even now, you can sympathise with the notion that two squirrels are better than one. The lesson, though, is that introducing new animals from other parts of the world is a guarantee that all will end in tears. There is now no chance that the grey squirrel will ever be eradicated from Britain, and the red will never return to its former glory.

What, though, is going to happen now? The first conclusion we should draw is that the red squirrel is likely to survive in Britain, despite a falling population, so long as climate change does not alter the mix of trees in the north. That is because large populations reside in Central Scotland, where they retreat into large conifer forests, a habitat that greys don't like as much. However, there are also a few signs of hope elsewhere.

Firstly, whatever you might think of controlling grey squirrels, it does seem to work in some places. There is a project called Red Squirrels United, which particularly works in areas where greys are moving into hitherto exclusively red zones, often carrying SQPV with them. Targeted removal of grey squirrels in these areas is stalling the march of the greys.

Intriguingly, there is another, unexpected, twist to the story. The pine marten is a major predator of red squirrels wherever they meet, and in Britain they have coexisted for thousands of years. The pine marten was once common throughout Britain, but by the 14th century deforestation had brought about a major decline, and after this the pine marten was heavily persecuted as vermin and finally eradicated from all but a redoubt in Scotland and Northern Ireland. However, persecution is now much reduced, and the pine marten is rapidly increasing.

Grey squirrels are fatter and heavier than red squirrels, and by consequence easier to catch. It turns out that, where the two overlap, pine martens are voracious predators of grey squirrels and have a major impact on their population. In parts of Ireland, the increase of pine martens has caused a decrease in grey squirrels and protected the red squirrel population. Pine martens have been widely reintroduced, including into the Forest of Dean, in Gloucestershire, where they are controlling grey squirrels very effectively.

The surge of pine martens now introduces a quite new dynamic. Although pine martens don't reach into suburban areas, it is now possible that in wilder areas the predator may be the saviour of its erstwhile favourite prey.

And it is truly ironic that by reintroducing one native, we might help another native in its ecological battle with an outsider.

Hazel Dormouse

Muscardinus avellanarius

--- FACT FILE ---

DISTRIBUTION

Formerly most of England and Wales,
but now mainly southern half of
England and Welsh border.

CURRENT STATUS

Vulnerable.

PAST AND CURRENT POPULATIONS

Past unknown, but common, probably
several million. Current 930,000.
Possible 48% drop in population
between 1995 and 2015.

DESCRIPTION OF THE SPECIES

6–9cm long, plus tail 6–7cm long.
Mouse-like with beautiful golden fur
and bushy tail, the latter as long as body.
Small black eyes and long whiskers.

DESCRIPTION OF THE THREATS

Loss of ancient woodland;
fragmentation of blocks of habitat.

WHAT WE NEED TO DO

Plant hedgerows between inhabited
woodlands; make a dormouse box;
adopt a dormouse.

ORGANISATIONS TO SUPPORT

People's Trust for Endangered Species
(PTES); Wildwood Trust.

CHANCES OF SURVIVAL
IN BRITAIN TO 2050

4/5

The hazel dormouse is an animal with such delicious good looks that it should be one of the most popular characters in Britain. The moment you join a dormouse box-check and meet it face to face in the wild for the first time, it is almost impossible not to exclaim: 'Oh isn't it sweet?' The hazel dormouse drips adorableness; it is quintessentially endearing.

The dormouse is also a fascinating little rodent. The name comes from the French word *dormir*, which means 'to sleep', and the dormouse is one of the few British mammals that hibernates, along with bats and hedgehogs. But this is an exceptional hibernation, an absolute marathon. Some animals sleep between October and April, or even May every year, which almost feels like slumbering your life away. One dormouse of a different species, the fat dormouse, has been recorded being inactive for 346 days in a row! When hibernating, which the hazel dormouse does in a nest on the ground, it actually wakes up every 30 days for a few hours, enough for a trip to the toilet and to catch up on emails. But its dedication to the snooze is such that, if the British summer night is too hot, it will drop off then too!

Being strictly nocturnal, and also largely arboreal, spending its active nights in trees and hedgerows well above ground, the dormouse should be rather a mysterious animal, far removed from human experience. But it isn't, its habits being well known to our forebears, which suggests that it must once have been abundant. It was found in almost every English county up until the 19th century, presumably at such a high density that people were able to become familiar with it.

That, though, was the high watermark of its population in Britain. It has been in decline ever since. It has now been lost from at least half its range. The only meaningful figures available, from the National Dormouse Monitoring Survey, suggest a 48% drop in population between 1995 and 2015. Its range continues to melt away.

The hazel dormouse faces a number of threats, but one of the most interesting ones is a problem that, when people think about conservation, doesn't usually immediately pop into their orbit. It's the problem of fragmentation. If dormice are lost from a wood, but still occur a mile away in another wood, their arboreal nature and lack of a wandering character means that they won't recolonise the first wood from the second, unless there is a corridor between one place and the other. One of the methods of dormouse conservation is to grow hedgerows to defragment the population so that they can come and go. Otherwise isolated populations become very vulnerable.

Another big problem for the dormouse is woodland management – which also, in itself, is another huge issue often overlooked by the general public, who might be aware of the dangers, for example, of agricultural intensification. Changes in woodland management over recent years have often had a negative effect on wildlife, such as the reduction in coppicing, in which trees such as hazel and sweet chestnut were regularly cut near the base to encourage shoots to grow out from the stump, providing straight sticks for fencing and other jobs. Coppices, with their dense, low, scrubby growth are ideal for dormice, but very little coppicing is done today, and what coppices that remain are often heavily browsed by Britain's excessive deer population.

The hazel dormouse thrives particularly well in ancient woodlands, as these have the highest density of rich plant food that a dormouse needs, such as flowers, pollen, fruits, berries and nuts. Ancient woods are the richest terrestrial habitats in the UK. They are defined as areas of woodland that have been woods since 1600, when accurate maps were first available in England, or 1750 in Scotland. Over time, centuries of accumulated dead wood and undisturbed soils make these places unique. Only 52,000 such sites remain in Britain, covering only 2.4% of the country.

Politicians and developers have long been blind to the significance of ancient woodlands, typified by one former environment secretary who notoriously managed to suggest that the loss of ancient woodland to housing and other development could be mitigated by planting trees elsewhere (well, it might in 400 years' time). This is also a reason for some of the conservationists' outcry over the HS2 project, which the Woodland Trust claims will impact on 108 ancient woodlands. Unfortunately, these are unique and irreplaceable habitats that once lost are lost forever.

All is not lost for the hazel dormouse, however. It is a species of high conservation concern and is a major study species for the People's Trust for Endangered Species (PTES), which has been running the National Dormouse Monitoring Scheme since 1990. The Trust also runs reintroduction schemes, hoping to replace populations that have been lost. Up until now it has introduced about 1,000 dormice into 24 sites. As mentioned above, dormice suffer from the fragmentation of their habitat, and the PTES are building up hedge highways all over the country to connect populations. They even build bridges to allow the mammals to cross new roads and other developments. Meanwhile, Natural England has a scheme to plant 30,000 hectares of woodland every year.

One of the best ways to help dormice is to put up boxes for them, in the same way that they help bird populations. You can tell it is a dormouse box if the entrance faces into the tree to which it is fixed, not out (see page 188).

If you want to help the dormice near you, you should join the PTES, and you could also contribute money to your nearest monitoring group to help pay for boxes. You can also adopt a dormouse via the Wildwood Trust website.

Bottlenose Dolphin

Tursiops truncatus

FACT FILE

DISTRIBUTION

Inshore waters of south-west England, Wales, Irish Sea and Hebrides; north-east England and Scotland; Northern Irish coast. Wanders offshore elsewhere.

CURRENT STATUS

Least Concern. Legally protected.

PAST AND CURRENT POPULATIONS

Past unknown. Currently a few hundred are resident in our waters.

DESCRIPTION OF THE SPECIES

1.9–3.9m long. Large dark-grey dolphin with short, stubby beak. Most often identified by its distinctive sickle-shaped dorsal fin. Playful and often leaps out of the water or bow-rides boats.

DESCRIPTION OF THE THREATS

Pollution; collisions with boats and other craft; changing fish stocks; discarded or used fishing tackle; underwater noise.

WHAT WE NEED TO DO

Regulate pleasure craft in suitable areas; cut all forms of pollution and overfishing; promote interest in marine environment; take part in a beach clean to reduce plastic in our seas — see page 208 or find your local beach clean event via the National Trust website; report sightings to MARINElife.

ORGANISATIONS TO SUPPORT

Marine Conservation Society; National Trust; Surfers Against Sewage; MARINElife.

CHANCES OF SURVIVAL IN BRITAIN TO 2050

5/5

There can be few animals that everyone adores, but dolphins must be one of them. Whether the feeling is mutual, we will never know. Dolphins are supremely intelligent masters of the sea, and they may have an opinion of us. If they do, they might not be impressed by how we treat our marine environment.

Many people are surprised when they hear that you can see wild dolphins in Britain, but you can, and it isn't particularly difficult to do so. In some parts of the country there are resident populations and you can take a boat out to find them, or even see them from land (Chanonry Point, on the Moray Firth near Inverness in Scotland is probably the most famous location). There are populations in Cardigan Bay, Cornwall, Northumberland and North Wales, as well as the Moray Firth, amounting to several hundred individuals. Dolphins can turn up anywhere else too.

The British Isles are remarkably rich in marine mammals. In addition to dolphins, we have porpoises, whales and many seals. When you realise what they have to put up with, though, you do wonder why they bother to live here. Dolphins are fiendishly difficult to count, and so there are no concrete figures to suggest how much they might have declined. However, populations in the English Channel and around the Humber Estuary have either disappeared or relocated.

There is little doubt that Britain's waters are not as rich for dolphins as they once were. Dolphins, like humans, eat fish and cephalopods (squids and octopuses), and many of these have been vastly depleted by overfishing. For example, haddock populations fell by 60% between 1990 and 2010 in the North Sea for a variety of reasons, including overfishing and an increase in sea temperatures. Cod numbers dropped by 39%, whiting by nearly 40% and sole by 39% in the same period. One cannot imagine how much all these fish, exploited by commercial trawling, must have been affected over the longer period, although it is estimated that, worldwide, 90% of all predatory fish stocks have gone. 80% of the world's fisheries are under pressure. With such a significant drop in many of its prey animals, the bottlenose dolphin must have suffered, too.

The pollution of the marine environment also makes life difficult for all our seafaring animals. In recent years the enormous increase in plastic in the ocean food chains has been exposed, and all this adds to the general littering from humankind. Oil spills, fuel dumping and discarded fishing tackle are all dangerous for dolphins. If they get entangled in fishing nets, they quickly die. You can help mitigate these problems by joining a beach clean (see page 208).

There are also some problems for dolphins that are more specific, and one of these is the potential for collision between marine mammals and high-speed craft. Not only is there much more shipping than there used to be, crafts are also going faster, including high-speed ferries, which travel in excess of 30 knots; nobody knows how well dolphins cope with these. For inshore species such as bottlenose dolphins, collisions with powerboats and other rapid pleasure craft are inevitable; unfortunately, many of these could lead to a slow, lingering death. People in unregulated craft are notorious for approaching dolphins too closely, seemingly oblivious to the fact that this can cause the animals stress.

One excellent development over the last few years has been a large increase in the number of people enjoying dolphin cruises and whale-watching trips. These not only delight people, but the best ones alert the attendees to the problems facing marine mammals, which can only be good – if they don't, you could give them feedback, such as on Tripadvisor or Facebook, to make sure they change. Please do attend one of these with a clear conscience. Around the UK there is a code of conduct (see details on MARINElife website) which forbids pleasure boats to approach any closer than 100m

(200m if there are two boats) and not to motor at speed towards them. Dolphins are curious animals and frequently approach boats and ride their bow waves, so sometimes this is unavoidable. However, if your operator neither informs you about the dolphins' plight nor adheres to the code, make sure you let them know you're on their case.

Another very specific problem for dolphins and whales in our oceans is the sound environment. Dolphins often hunt in the murky depths, where little light penetrates and they cannot use their eyesight. Instead they rely on echolocation, emitting high-frequency sounds that bounce back and paint an aural picture of their environment. It happens so quickly that they can pursue and catch fast-moving fish without seeing them until the last moment. Echolocation is also useful for communicating between individuals.

Compared to 100 years ago, the sea is a very noisy place and, unfortunately, many human sounds overlap in frequency with the dolphins' sonar-like pulses. The propellers of ships and other craft must make the environment very loud and annoying for them. Military operations sometimes use very loud pulses, which could potentially inhibit a dolphin's ability to carry out its daily tasks.

We might not be able to intervene in military operations, but there is still plenty we can do for dolphins and other marine animals, even if we live far from the coast. Being careful about litter and waste will prevent unwanted detritus reaching the seas, and we can make sure that household and care products we use are as environmentally friendly as possible. We can also be careful about the fish we eat, ensuring that it is acquired sustainably. If we do live in a coastal community we can lobby for good practice among water sports enthusiasts. And if we are fortunate enough to own or hire pleasure craft, especially of the faster variety, we owe it to these delightful animals, which are close to us in sheer intelligence, to go carefully.

Wildcat

Felis silvestris

FACT FILE

DISTRIBUTION

A few parts of the Scottish Highlands. Uses a tapestry of habitats including forest, moorland, mountains.

CURRENT STATUS

Critically Endangered.

PAST AND CURRENT POPULATIONS

Once widespread all over Britain. Now a very optimistic maximum of 200.

DESCRIPTION OF THE SPECIES

47–66cm long, with tail an extra 26–33cm. Most similar to a stripy tabby cat, but larger and more muscular. Has thick tail with rounded black tip; dark dorsal stripe doesn't extend down tail.

DESCRIPTION OF THE THREATS

Persecution and habitat loss, but now mainly hybridisation with domestic cats.

WHAT WE NEED TO DO

Pray. Isolate any reasonably pure stock from domestic cats; captive breeding and releases; report any possible wildcat sightings.

ORGANISATIONS TO SUPPORT

Mammal Society; Scottish Wildcat Action; Saving Wildcats.

CHANCES OF SURVIVAL IN BRITAIN TO 2050

1/5

A genuine wildcat is far removed from the animal that sits on your lap, purring. True, your household feline is closely related to the wildcat, but it is genetically distinct. The wildcat is like a house cat on steroids – bigger, more aggressive, not at all tame and not at all at home in human company. This is an animal that easily survives the Scottish winter and kills rabbits as well as the usual rodents and birds. It is tough and resourceful.

However, no amount of resourcefulness is likely to save our wildcat. Now limited to tiny numbers in Scotland, it is very close to the precipice of localised extinction. Fortunately, it still survives well in Europe and Asia, but the cats of Britain have been isolated from the rest for about 9,000 years. They aren't genetically isolated enough to be an official subspecies, but hey, they are ours!

It is extraordinary to think that the wildcat once roamed throughout the UK, but in the Middle Ages it was heavily hunted, and this was also a time of intense deforestation. By the 16th century it had disappeared from southern England, and it was eliminated from the rest of England and Wales by 1880. It has been rare for quite some time now, but there is probably enough habitat for a reasonable population to survive in Scotland. True, the notorious owners of some Scottish estates probably sanction some illegal hunting, but the reason that the wildcat is on the brink of extinction is a very different one.

The villain of this piece is the feral cat. Feral cats are abandoning their human homes and firesides, venturing into the Scottish countryside and cross-breeding with the wildcat. This has been going on for such a long time that very few, if any, wildcats on the loose in Scotland are completely genetically pure.

You might argue whether this matters, but the wildcat is a genuine member of our fauna, with its own ecological place and history, and the domestic cat is a separate species that probably originated in the Near East. It is an interloper. The Scottish wildcat is a symbol of Scotland and of many Scottish clans. They admire its fierce nature.

Whether or not you agree that cross-breeding the wildcat out of an independent existence is a bad thing or a storm in a teacup, there can be little doubt that, from a conservation viewpoint at least, feral cats are very bad news in the British countryside. Argue all you like about the destruction wrought by domestic cats (100 million wild animals a year), the fact that we have a potentially substantial number of free-range cats with heightened need to hunt is a scandal. Some estimates put the number at 1.5 million. These are abandoned, uncontrolled professional hunters at large in our countryside.

As for the Scottish wildcat, there are serious conservation measures being rolled out to save it, and we can only hope for their success. There are captive breeding programmes afoot and Scottish Wildcat Action has outlined five areas of Scotland for a programme including preserving wild areas, neutering the local feral cats and removing any feral cats that might carry contagious diseases. On the isolated Ardnamurchan Peninsula they are doing all this and neutering the local domestic cats as well.

It might be too little too late. Keeping wildcats isolated from feral cats that have already gone wild feels like an impossible ask. A report commissioned by Scottish Wildcat Action recently suggested that numbers of true wildcats are already too low to be viable. However, it is worth persevering, and all the agencies working with this animal deserve our support. Perhaps the only way forward is to catch the last of the remaining population and breed them in captivity, building up a population and then releasing them back into the wild. But even this won't solve the problem of feral cats – unless, of course, large areas of rewilded Scotland become available once again.

What the fate of the wildcat does show us is that, when animals are introduced from elsewhere, it is often a serious problem. So, if you have a cat at home, keep it there!

Nightingale

Luscinia megarhynchos

FACT FILE

DISTRIBUTION

Localised in south-east and southern England, in tall scrub and woodland edge. Summer visitor April—August.

CURRENT STATUS

Red Listed as a Species of Conservation Concern.

PAST AND CURRENT POPULATIONS

Once commoner, but populations weren't estimated until recently. Currently 6,700 singing males.

DESCRIPTION OF THE SPECIES

15—16.5cm long. A small brown bird with a loud voice. Like robin in shape but slightly longer tail and lacks any orange. Rusty-brown on rump and tail. Dark eye.

DESCRIPTION OF THE THREATS

Destruction of current habitats; fewer coppices; deer grazing; less habitat on wintering grounds.

WHAT WE NEED TO DO

Strong protection for remaining sites where it occurs; favourable management.

ORGANISATIONS TO SUPPORT

Wildlife Trusts; Royal Society for the Protection of Birds (RSPB); Nightingale Nights.

CHANCES OF SURVIVAL IN BRITAIN TO 2050

4/5

L ook at a photograph of a nightingale and you won't be impressed; listen to one, however, and you will be astonished. Hear one in the wild, and life won't ever be the same again.

The nightingale is a small, brown bird. It is related to the robin but lacks all the charm of the garden icon and is very plain to look at. It isn't in any way tame and wouldn't dream of doing anything so common as to perch on a spade. It is not found in close proximity to people, but only in certain types of scrubby woodland. It doesn't seem to be a great fan of our country, each year arriving in April, falling silent in May and leaving in August, returning to Africa for the winter.

Yet the nightingale is a national and international treasure. The song is melodious, rich and thrilling, with an astonishing dynamic range, from a whisper to a shout. Every male sings its own individual song. The song first grabs you, then charms you, then amazes you. It is heard at the most romantic time of the year, deep spring, an accompaniment to the happy delirium of verdant green, sweet blossom and increasing daylight. The poet John Milton declared as long ago as the 1630s that the nightingale was the bird of lovers. Writing in Vienna, Beethoven celebrated it as a pastoral bird familiar to all in his sixth symphony in 1808.

The prevalence of the nightingale in British culture points to an abundance of the species that is long past. The English poet John Keats wrote his melancholic 'Ode to a Nightingale' in 1819 after hearing an individual on Hampstead Heath, London, from where it is long gone. By the time the wartime classic 'A Nightingale Sang in Berkeley Square' was written in 1939, the idea of the iconic songster singing in London was pure whimsy. The world-famous cellist Beatrice Harrison played to accompany a wild

nightingale in Oxted, Surrey in 1924 (the world's first wildlife outside broadcast on the radio in Britain), a county in which the bird just about hangs on, mainly in the south.

We can only estimate how common the nightingale was historically. It was present over a large swathe of southern England until the beginning of the 20th century. In recent years, however, its numbers and range have begun to contract seriously, starting in the 1980s. Between 1995 and 2016 the British nightingale population dropped by 59%, and it is estimated that the last 50 years has brought about a reduction of a terrifying 93%. There are now only a few thousand singing males in the country each spring; even more worryingly, it is also declining on the Continent, where the nightingale has until recently been a very common bird.

Be in no doubt, the nightingale is in serious trouble. Unfortunately, the precise causes are subtle and still not entirely clear. One issue is likely to be on its wintering grounds in Africa, where the humid tropical forest in countries such as Senegal, Sierra Leone and Guinea is slowly being degraded or destroyed. There isn't much we can do about that.

Another problem is that nightingales are particularly fond of coppices, a type of traditional woodland management that involves cutting trees at the stump so that they send out new shoots that are ideal in girth for fences and other structures. The practice of coppicing has little commercial value now, so it tends to be up to conservation organisations or sympathetic landowners to keep it going. The birds are fussy enough to require a certain age of coppice, too, which has some bare ground below the trees but enough thick scrub to protect the ground-based nests. Deer, especially muntjac, need to be kept out by fences, because they chew away at the scrub that the songsters need. All in all, it usually takes expensive management to keep nightingale numbers high anywhere.

Most people, though, who have heard the bird singing in the wild would agree that it is a price worth paying. That's why, as ever, subscriptions to the Wildlife Trusts, RSPB and other conservation organisations are so helpful (see page 239). You can also help nightingales directly by helping with coppicing work and other conservation tasks; volunteer your services to any nature reserve with nightingales near you, or to the Wildlife Trusts.

In the wider world, the nightingale is unfortunately most densely concentrated in the south of England, where myriad interests compete for space. This means that several woods and scrubby areas where the birds occur are at threat of development. The most famous example is in Kent, at Lodge Hill, where a former Ministry of Defence site has, by natural regeneration, been recast into the most important area for the nightingale in

Britain, with 66 singing males. It is an incredible place, with important grassland areas, too, simply buzzing with life. It is also, mercifully, free of deer. In 2013 it was declared a Site of Special Scientific Interest (SSSI), a strong designation for the finest areas for wildlife in the UK.

This is not enough, however, to protect it from development, and Medway Council agreed outline planning permission for the building of 5,000 new homes on the site in 2014, along with schools and a hotel. This was despite opposition from a planning inspector, many local councillors and several conservation groups. It was argued that no other large brownfield site existed locally that could provide much needed housing. Pressure by central government – whose own inadequacies over the years have never come close to solving Britain's housing shortage – now places heavy pressure upon any number of councils to cave in to development demands.

Up until now, campaigns by the RSPB and other groups have managed to stall the complete destruction of Lodge Hill. In December 2018 Homes England, the owners, reduced the plan to 500 houses, none of which was on the area designated as an SSSI. However, building such a significant housing estate close to nightingale habitat still threatens the birds. Domestic cats could easily wander into the area and destroy the nests.

The battle between the world's greatest songbird and yet another soulless housing estate is a battle for the soul of our country. The nation needs nature and nightingales. There should never have been the slightest chance that such an enchanted place should have been built upon, especially one with the legal protection of an SSSI. The fact it needed to be fought is a sad indictment of our country's priorities.

If you do happen to live in a nightingale area, do be on the lookout for creeping development. Local councils produce news of planning applications, so sign up for these.

Hen Harrier

Circus cyaneus

FACT FILE

DISTRIBUTION

Breeds widely on moors on Scottish mainland, Orkney, northern England and Wales, the Isle of Man and parts of Ireland. May winter in southern parts of England.

CURRENT STATUS

Red Listed as a Species of Conservation Concern. Near Threatened in Europe.

PAST AND CURRENT POPULATIONS

Never properly assessed until recently. Currently 780 pairs, including Ireland. There was a 9% decline between 2010 and 2016. In Scotland there was a 20% decline between 2004 and 2010.

DESCRIPTION OF THE SPECIES

45–55cm long, with a wingspan of 99–121cm. Quite large raptor with owl-like face, long, narrow wings, held up in a V when flying slowly, and a long tail. Smaller male is smoky-grey with black wingtips. Female brown with obvious white rump, dark rings on tail.

DESCRIPTION OF THE THREATS

Illegal persecution.

WHAT WE NEED TO DO

Stop illegal persecution; licensing grouse moors.

ORGANISATIONS TO SUPPORT

RSPB.

CHANCES OF SURVIVAL IN BRITAIN TO 2050

2/5

54

This is currently the great soap opera of wildlife conservation. The story has everything: political intrigue, organised crime, class warfare, money, power and stardust.

At the centre is the hen harrier, a magnificent bird of prey that breeds on upland heather moorland. Long-winged and long-tailed, in spring it performs an incredible aerial display of sweeping and swooping at high altitude, a sky-dance of breathtaking beauty. It hunts by flying slowly over open ground, catching what it flushes. Once found

widely across the uplands of northern England and Scotland, its population has shrunk in recent years. An independent government report recently concluded that northern England has room for 300 pairs of harriers and Scotland 1,500. Instead of this, in 2016 a count reported fewer than 20 pairs in England and 460 pairs in Scotland. The picture improved in England in 2020, with 60 chicks fledging from 24 monitored nests.

The uplands are obviously suffering from hen harrier deficit disorder, to the tune of at least 1,300 pairs. Why? All available evidence points to their illegal trapping, poisoning and shooting. The finger is pointed at estates that are managed for grouse shooting.

These estates operate by doing everything they can to ensure that the red grouse breed well each year on their heather moorlands. During the shooting season, lasting from the 'Glorious Twelfth' of August to 10 December, groups of beaters will regularly need to drive high numbers of birds towards lines of paying hunters. The grouse are fast flyers, providing a difficult target, but if there are enough birds, just about anyone can bag a grouse flying over. The attractive scenery, tradition and sporting value make grouse shooting a high-value activity for the moor owners. Clients are generally wealthy.

They are also demanding. If the grouse numbers are low, the season could be cancelled, owing to dissatisfied customers not getting their money's worth. This means that any factors that reduce red grouse densities are a problem. And there are quite a few problems, not least hen harriers. These are known to feed on red grouse chicks, and a recent study suggested that they can reduce red grouse abundance by 50%. As far as grouse-moor owners are concerned, that crosses a red line.

It is hardly surprising, therefore, that at least some moorland owners and their staff are tempted to persecute hen harriers, as well as other birds of prey, such as golden eagles, that might also take the odd grouse. The only problem is that hen harriers and eagles have been legally protected since 1954, and any persecution also crosses a line.

Up to this point, the story adds up to an understandable conflict of interest. Unfortunately, however, the moorland owners and their apologists, who include the odd sporting celebrity, have unwisely taken a path of denial. They claim that they don't persecute hen harriers or other birds of prey, instead blaming rogue elements. They have even accused the RSPB and other conservation bodies of dishonesty in providing evidence of illegal persecution.

Their words and claims don't seem to stack up. In recent years, many young hen harriers have been fitted with satellite tags. Since 2018, of 39 tagged harriers that have been killed or have disappeared in Scotland, 27 have met their fate either on a grouse moor or adjacent to one. In 2017, not a single hen harrier chick was raised on a grouse moor, despite the vast areas of suitable habitat. Perhaps even more damning is the fact that most birds of prey in Britain have thrived under protection, recovering after persecution became illegal. Marsh harriers, red kites and buzzards are good examples, all doing well elsewhere.

Some grouse-moor owners continue to resist regulation and openness. Up to the present, any convictions for raptor persecution have been as rare as the harriers themselves, amounting to one solitary instance. This suggests that in some areas there may be local resistance to cooperating with law enforcement. The systematic killing of protected birds, together with a wall of silence, is nothing less than organised crime.

Had the owners been cooperative and open, allowing regulation and other measures, some kind of accommodation might well have been reached between the estates and conservationists. And to be fair, for their own part, conservationists have often veered unnecessarily towards outrage and combustibility. The general public tends to be understanding about a person's right to use their own land as they wish. Obfuscation and denial, however, has put the industry on a sticky wicket. It has helped to put a spotlight on the wider issues of grouse moors and their environmental standards, and they don't come out well.

Conservationists, led by the brave battering-ram Mark Avery and fuelled by the stardust of TV star Chris Packham, point out that raptor persecution isn't the only destruction on grouse moors. Quite legally, many hundreds of other carnivores, including foxes and stoats, are also systematically controlled. A League Against Cruel Sports field study has suggested that 250,000 animals are killed each year to support the industry. These include, controversially, mountain hares, which thrive on grouse moors, but are culled to the tune of 26,000 every year. Only in 2020 did this become subject to licence in Scotland. The hares can carry a tick-borne virus that in theory could be passed to red grouse. This has never been proven in the wild. Sheep and deer could transmit the same virus. Not surprisingly, there has been an outcry.

That's not all. Grouse-moor husbandry also includes regular rotational burning of moorland each April to ensure that there is a wide variety of age stands of heather and to provide green shoots of heather regrowth for the young grouse to eat. Heather-burning is damaging for biodiversity and the general health of the environment, partly by reducing the moisture content of the peat.

It is hard not to conclude that grouse moors are bad for the environment and promote wildlife crime. However, the owners point out that the grouse-shooting industry brings in much-needed money for struggling local communities. They also point out, correctly, that legal predator control can help other wildlife, such as breeding waders.

Grouse moors in Britain cover about 8% of our land area. In turn, they are thought to generate 2,600 jobs and about £67 million to local economies, which is about 0.005% of GDP. This is an overestimate of their worth, because they are also funded by government subsidies; the land is legally considered to be agricultural grazing land. So, quite apart from the other issues, the economics aren't impressive either. By contrast, in Scotland alone, nature-based tourism is estimated to produce £1.4 billion per year, along with almost 40,000 jobs.

In modern Britain, the wind is blowing. We like our civil liberties, with the result that we allow people to manage shooting for their estates. We might find the idea of well-heeled people paying already very wealthy landowners to provide 'sport' somewhat distasteful, but we tolerate it. However, to do so pays a very high environmental price on our uplands, a bill to which we all contribute, and stretches that tolerance to the limit. Then we hear brazen denials that they are breaking the law of the land to ensure the very rich have enough grouse to kill. At this point, perhaps, society's patience is exhausted.

On the other hand, the future of our uplands also depends on a sensible accommodation with landowners, many of whom harbour genuine environmental concerns. The best solution is dialogue between the two sides, and an understanding that no perfect solution exists.

There are numerous ways to support hen harriers and stop their persecution, apart from the usual conservation organisations such as the RSPB and Wildlife Trusts. You may wish to lobby the National Trust (and National Trust for Scotland), which allows grouse shooting on some of its land. To get a balanced look at the issues, check out the views of the following:

> Mark Avery's blog – everyone should follow this courageous conservation hero's blog. You don't always have to agree with him. He organises petitions and other campaigns.
>
> Raptor Persecution UK – very much against grouse shooting.
>
> Moorland Association – the other side of the story.
>
> Game and Wildlife Conservation Trust.

Swift

Apus apus

FACT FILE

DISTRIBUTION

Throughout the UK, often in towns and cities. A summer visitor, arriving in late April and leaving in August.

CURRENT STATUS

Amber Listed as Species of Conservation Concern.

PAST AND CURRENT POPULATIONS

Distant past unknown. Latest estimate 59,000 pairs in 2016, down 53% from 1995.

DESCRIPTION OF THE SPECIES

17–18.5cm long, wingspan 40–44cm. Aerial bird with long, narrow, swept-back wings. Mainly dark brown with white throat. Has forked tail, but head protrudes less than swallow's. Never perches on wires.

DESCRIPTION OF THE THREATS

Fewer flying insects; fewer nest sites. Pesticides in air circulation.

WHAT WE NEED TO DO

Widespread provision of swift boxes; build swift bricks into new housing estates; record swifts seen near nesting places by members of the public using the Swift Mapper app.

ORGANISATIONS TO SUPPORT

Swift Conservation; RSPB; British Trust for Ornithology (BTO).

CHANCES OF SURVIVAL IN BRITAIN TO 2050

4/5

Swifts in this country face two main threats. One of these we can do a lot about ourselves and make a genuine personal contribution in our back garden or local area. The other threat we can just tremble about.

The swift is an extraordinary bird that, for much of its life, is entirely aerial. It looks like the better-known swallow, but is slightly bigger, with much thinner wings that are slender at the base and sharply pointed, giving the bird a sickle-like shape. Swallows often perch on wires and other things, but the remarkable swift never does this, because it cannot perch, only cling to vertical surfaces. The upshot is that, except for breeding, it hardly ever lands anywhere at all.

Think about that for a moment. At the end of the breeding season, the swift departs from Britain in August and flies to Africa; it doesn't return here until late April or May. During all that time it probably never lands, so that means that it flies for at least eight months without stopping. How does it sleep, you might wonder? The answer is amazing. It sleeps half its brain at a time, first one hemisphere and then the other. It probably only naps for short periods of time, but this seems to be enough for it.

That is only half the amazing story of the swift. It undertakes an epic migration. It leaves our shores, flies over France, Spain and North Africa and settles over the Congo Basin, where it pauses for a few months. Then, not content with its 5,000km journey, it then tracks east as far as the Indian Ocean, then back again, following local concentrations of flying insects. It doesn't make its way straight back, but crosses the Gulf of Guinea to the rainforests of West Africa, for example in Liberia, before finally tracking up through North Africa and Spain to our shores. Its overall migration encompasses at least 30,000km of travel, and it probably never stops flying, even for a moment.

Swifts do something else extraordinary, too. Their primary food is flying insects, the so-called 'aeroplankton' that drifts on summer breezes above treetop height, and is made up from untold millions of small flying insects, such as aphids and flies, and even tiny spiders riding high on strands of web, parachute-like. On settled summer days this food is abundant, and when conditions are ideal a swift may deliver a 'ball' of 1,000 or more separate items to its young. However, when a weather front is approaching the available food nosedives, and adult swifts may opt to fly away from their nest and young and fly right away from the area. They might even circumnavigate the weather front, sometimes travelling for hundreds of kilometres, even away from British airspace. Meanwhile the young stick it out in the nest, looking forward to the adults' return. Fortunately, young swifts are adapted to cope with periods of starvation.

From the above, it will be obvious how critical the supply of flying insects is to a swift and its young. It should also be obvious that if swifts are doing badly over a long period of time, that is likely to be the result of insect populations also declining. There is scientific evidence that insect numbers are falling everywhere. Chemical pesticides used widely in farming and gardening are likely to be part of the problem.

If the latter is happening on a large scale, we should be gravely worried. Flying insects aren't quite the air that we breathe, but they depend on it, and any harm done to them is being done to us.

And, unfortunately, swift populations are tumbling. Between 1995 and 2016 they have dropped by 53% over the whole country.

However, there is a second reason for seeing fewer swifts about the place, and happily this is something in which we can intervene. For thousands of years, swifts have nested in buildings, using cavities at a reasonable height – not too low, because swifts cannot take off if they are accidentally grounded. Up until recently, swifts used the multiple ledges and cavities found on old buildings. Nowadays, though, building regulations have changed, ensuring that walls and roofs are sealed off. This means no access for swifts. Renovation of social housing has been a particular problem, as well as refurbishing of historic buildings. If this goes on in the breeding season, the swifts are sometimes prevented from reaching their own nests. When this happens, swifts can be killed or injured trying to get in.

There are cheap and sustainable solutions to this problem. Swifts are perfectly content to use purpose-designed boxes, which can easily be fitted to the sides of buildings, close to where the birds nested previously. You can also try to attract swifts to a completely new area. Swift boxes are widely available. There are several designs to choose from, from single boxes to quadruple, and since swifts usually nest in small colonies these are ideal. The cheapest are less than £20 and the most expensive more than £100, so there is some flexibility. You can also fit boxes with cameras, and even mounted swift towers. These are all available from the Swift Conservation website.

If you're not aware of swifts in your immediate neighbourhood, it's a great idea to use calls to attract them. These are also available from Swift Conservation, in CD and MP3 format. The screaming sounds are not at all annoying; your neighbours probably won't even notice them.

A new invention to help the birds has recently become available: the ingenious purpose-built swift brick or swift block. This is a hollow block that provides a home for swifts (and often house sparrows too) and can be built into a brick or rendered cavity wall, so can be added as part of a building project. The beauty of swift boxes is that they are inconspicuous, looking just like holes in the sides of buildings, and you can put in one or two, or a whole colony's worth. Swifts are themselves discreet and leave very little mess. If all new housing estates included swift bricks, much of this bird's decline would be halted in its tracks. It's mainly a matter of will. Several local councils are enthusiastically installing swift boxes in some of their major building projects. This trickle should become a flood.

Finally, if you see a screaming party of swifts in your area, make sure you alert the RSPB. You can install the Swift Mapper app on many devices. If conservation organisations know where the birds are, they can try to help them. Look out for council plans for new developments (many councils have newsletters for these). If your own house was built by one of the larger builders (or even if it wasn't), you can lobby the companies to help swifts. After all, you can but ask, and this can raise awareness.

Turtle Dove

Streptopelia turtur

FACT FILE

DISTRIBUTION

East and south-east England. A summer visitor from April to September.

CURRENT STATUS

Red Listed as a Species of Conservation Concern. Rated as Vulnerable by IUCN for Europe and Worldwide.

PAST AND CURRENT POPULATIONS

Down 98% on plots since 1970. In 2019, just over 1,000 pairs.

DESCRIPTION OF THE SPECIES

25–28cm long, wingspan 45–50cm. Small dove with long tail, 'pearl necklace' at its tip. Gloriously rich tortoiseshell pattern on the wings and back; zebra-crossing neck patch. Flies with flicking wingbeats.

DESCRIPTION OF THE THREATS

Lack of weed seeds during breeding season owing to agricultural intensification; shooting on migration; less available habitat in winter.

WHAT WE NEED TO DO

Ban on all hunting of this species properly policed; kinder regime on farms where it occurs; rewilding (see page 228).

ORGANISATIONS TO SUPPORT

RSPB; Operation Turtle Dove.

CHANCES OF SURVIVAL IN BRITAIN TO 2050

1/5

Within the next decades, it is quite likely that we will lose the turtle dove from Britain. If this happens, we will lose part of our soul. Yes, it is only a dove, a relative of mere pigeons, and it is so rare now that most people won't notice that it has gone. But over the millennia, turtle doves have visited Britain in summer. They were here as the countryside opened up in Neolithic times and would have flown over Stonehenge as it was being built. They were here when Roman legions marched across our hinterland. Chaucer wrote about them in the 14th century, admiring their marital faithfulness, then Shakespeare mentioned the same trait, albeit in mournful style in *The Winter's Tale*, published in 1623, perhaps alluding to the bird's gentle, slightly mournful soporific purr. Up until the two World Wars they were still a common bird, and even at the end of the 1960s were familiar over much of England.

But since 1970, the turtle dove population has declined by a barely credible 98%, the steepest rate of decline of any bird in Britain, perhaps the world. If anything, the tragedy is getting worse. Numbers dropped by 51% between 2012 and 2018.

If the situation was bad in Britain but less worrying in Europe, that would be consolation of a sort. In Europe as a whole, though, the turtle dove has lost 73% of its numbers between 1980 and 2010. This is pretty catastrophic and you might think that steps would be taken to mitigate the fall. How, then, can you explain that in July 2020 France's Minister of Ecological Transition allowed the powerful French shooting lobby to take out 17,460 turtle doves that autumn? The minister made a shuddering U-turn after an outcry, but the fact that such slaughter was ever contemplated is telling. To give you context, the British population is 1,000 pairs.

As mentioned several times in this book, I am quite sure that one day people will look back collectively at this sort of thing open-mouthed and wonder how the widespread slaughter of defenceless and vulnerable migrant birds could be considered a valid 'hobby' in the 21st century. The hunters argue that it is an important part of their culture and heritage. Maybe, but the spring arrival of turtle doves to the Middle East is mentioned in the Bible, in the Song of Songs, a piece that could date from the 3rd century BC. Is this not heritage?

There is little doubt that the turtle dove's epic migration, which takes it south over the Gallic and Spanish guns and into the Sahel region to the south of the Sahara, is an Achilles heel for it ecologically. And to be fair, it was not long ago that people trapped and killed turtle doves for much-needed food while the birds were following their migratory pathways. These days, however, the wholesale slaughter of doves (and all birds) that takes place in Mediterranean countries in autumn is unsustainable. Much is also illegal under widely ignored EU regulations. The last figures available put the turtle dove slaughter at 2–3 million birds in EU member states in 2007. The fact that the EU allows for extensive shooting of any vulnerable migratory birds is nothing less than an international scandal.

It seems that the turtle doves' winter refuge has changed, too, and not for the better. The birds winter in open woodland, especially around *Acacia* trees and, with the human population rapidly rising in the Sahel, there is pressure on woodland to be converted to agriculture, and overgrazing also affect the doves' habitat. Almost unbelievably some

European hunters, not content with taking pot shots at helpless birds in their own countries, now travel to the Sahel to do the same. Honestly, what kind of world do we live in?

It's true that that same human world includes many who care about turtle dove conservation. Whilst we should shout in the corridors of power about the shooting of migrants, there is much less we can do about our birds in Africa. However, when it comes to our own country, where the turtle dove also confronts difficulties, we can at least champion those who are doing something.

Here at home the turtle dove is declining in the face of a typical foe of lowland farms – intensive agriculture. Turtle doves feed entirely on seeds, especially of the weeds such as common fumitory, which dot the edges of fields. These are the cast-off flowers, the edge-of-society blooms, the unintentional botanical chaff. As farming has become efficient, the little patches of unloved mess have disappeared. Weeds have been poisoned, edges have become straighter, hedgerows (where the birds nest) torn down, meadows put under the plough. Our arable farmland is one of the most nature-depleted landscapes in the world.

Once, turtle doves would settle into the British countryside and produced two broods of two eggs. Nowadays they rarely get past the first family, probably because of a lack of food. Overall, they are producing half the number of chicks, on average, that they did in the 1970s. This statistic alone could account for the decline in Britain.

If you are reading this, what can you do to help? First and foremost, you can join any campaigns to stop the shooting of turtle doves in the Mediterranean – follow the Twitter feed CABS (Committee Against Bird Slaughter). You can even join groups that go out to places where birds are shot to try to stop the illegal poaching. Why not get involved with Operation Turtle Dove here at home. Visit reserves and rewilding estates, such as Knepp, which turtle doves inhabit. If you are fortunate enough to own land in turtle dove country, the RSPB will advise how you can help the birds. If enough people get on this gorgeous bird's bandwagon, there is still hope.

Puffin

Fratercula arctica

FACT FILE

DISTRIBUTION

Rocky coasts and offshore islands, mainly in the west and north.

CURRENT STATUS

Red Listed as a UK Bird of Conservation Concern; listed as Vulnerable by the IUCN.

PAST AND CURRENT POPULATIONS

1985–88: 488,700 apparently occupied burrows (AOB); 1998–2000: 580,000 AOB. Assumed much lower now.

DESCRIPTION OF THE SPECIES

28–34cm in length. Pigeon-sized seabird with upright stance, black above and white below, with red legs. Has white face and outsize, laterally flattened colourful bill.

DESCRIPTION OF THE THREATS

Climate change; overfishing; pollution.

WHAT WE NEED TO DO

Join the RSPB's Puffarazzi; lobby.

ORGANISATIONS TO SUPPORT

RSPB.

CHANCES OF SURVIVAL IN BRITAIN TO 2050

5/5

Everybody loves puffins, and for many people seeing a wild puffin is on their 'bucket list'. Perhaps surprisingly, this is quite an easy experience to tick off in the UK, if you travel to a sea-cliff or rocky island in parts of the west and north between April and July. Amazingly, Britain holds 10% of all the Atlantic puffins in the world and, just to stretch your credulity further, there are far more puffins breeding here (580,000 pairs) than that classic 'seagull', the herring gull (140,000 pairs).

These are birds that don't disappoint. In contrast to that actor or sportsperson who turns out to lack the friendly, dazzling personality you're expecting, the puffin is everything you hope for, and more. It is colourful, comical, unusual and characterful. It is often described as clown-like, and when you see it walking about, or trying to fly with its over-fast wingbeats and poor aerodynamics, the description fits. In some places, such as Skomer in Wales and the Farne Islands in Northumberland, you can walk around almost with puffins at your feet, and get to know them well. If you are ever fortunate enough to see an adult fly into its nesting burrow with a bill full of fish, held crosswise, you are privileged indeed.

Although there are many puffins in Britain, the big numbers are highly concentrated into a relatively small number of colonies. St Kilda, the outlying archipelago of the Western Isles, holds nearly half, with 250,000 pairs, while the Shetlands hold at least 100,000, the Farne Islands in Northumberland 40,000 and the Isle of May, off the Fife coast, 40,000. Skomer, an island in Wales, is home to 6,000. They are notoriously difficult to count, though, because the birds that are breeding are either in their burrows, or out at sea fishing. After breeding, the puffin lives a mysterious life, poorly known to scientists. From August to March the birds are all out at sea, seemingly spread out and difficult to find, riding out winter storms far from shore.

Until recently, the puffin would not have been a bird to worry about at all, breeding in remote colonies and wintering in even more remote seas. But all the signs are that this most popular of seabirds is declining. On Fair Isle, between Shetland and Orkney, the colonies have been carefully monitored, and show a 50% fall in population between 1986 and 2016. In Iceland, the headquarters of the world population, numbers have fallen from 7 million to 5.4 million. The declines are so alarming that the Atlantic puffin's official conservation designation is Vulnerable. They are Red Listed in the UK as a species of conservation concern.

Just as it is difficult to measure the population of puffins, it is even trickier to discern the reasons why numbers are falling. We need to know, though, because puffins are telling us something about the state of our seas. The puffin is the house sparrow of the oceans, a species once thought invulnerable but now showing signs of frailty. It is the canary of the seas, to stretch the metaphor even more. Researchers have clues as to why puffins are declining, and these clues are alarming.

The main problem is that the puffins' food of choice, the sand eel, is highly sensitive to environmental change. Warming seas have altered the distribution of these small fish. This is of prime importance, because during the breeding season puffins fly to and from their colonies, bringing back food for their young. Puffins are long-lived birds, frequently reaching 20 years or more in age, and they are faithful to their breeding colonies and nest-sites year after year. If warming seas mean that the sand eels change distribution, the puffins cannot easily adapt if these are suddenly out of reach. They might still be able to find them, but the longer journey may mean that they cannot get enough food to the pufflings. They can eat other fish, but sand eels are usually abundant where found.

That isn't the only known problem for puffins. Overfishing is also a problem. Sand eels aren't eaten by people, but they are fished for animal feed and fertiliser. In 2002 the population crashed. Anchovy stocks have done much the same. Puffins eat some of the fish that we catch too, such as sprats and herrings, which can be a standby if sand eels are not available. As mentioned above, puffins frequently nest in large, densely packed colonies. If a disaster afflicts a colony, such as an oil spill or other polluting event, many seabirds, including puffins, may suffer devastating losses and can take years to recover. They only produce a single chick a year and take about six years to mature, so it takes a long time to recruit a youngster into the breeding population. Puffins are also vulnerable to ground predators such as rats or cats, so if any of these were to arrive for the first time at a colony, this could be similarly disastrous.

What, though, can we do about the potential fate of the puffin? Some of the breeding colonies are looked after by the RSPB and other organisations, so a visit to one of these will benefit the birds themselves. Buying sustainably sourced fish to eat helps, as do the various ways that you don't add too much plastic waste and pollution to the sea, such as cutting down on plastic and chemicals in the home. Although this is one of those animals that only the professional conservationists can do much about, you can still help by lobbying government to make marine environments more sustainable. So far, the government has delineated 50 Marine Conservation Zones around the British Isles, but as yet none affect seabirds or sand eels.

You can also help by lobbying the government of Iceland to stop the practice of catching puffins for food (see page 231 for more advice on lobbying). The RSPB is also asking people to join the Puffarazzi (love it!), submitting photos of puffins bringing in food to the young, and including location details.

Skylark

Alauda arvensis

FACT FILE

DISTRIBUTION

Throughout Britain and Ireland all year round.

CURRENT STATUS

Red Listed as a Species of Conservation Concern.

PAST AND CURRENT POPULATIONS

3 million territories in early 1980s. Dropped by 54% since 1980s to 1.5 million territories and halved again during the 1990s.

DESCRIPTION OF THE SPECIES

16–18cm long. Streaky brown bird with obvious crest, slightly smaller than a starling, with white outer tail feathers and whitish trailing edge to wings. Walks on the ground, perches on fence posts. Most often seen in hovering song-flight high above the ground.

DESCRIPTION OF THE THREATS

Farming intensification, particularly the switch from spring sown to autumn sown cereals; higher stocking rates in fields; fewer stubbles.

WHAT WE NEED TO DO

Widely applied skylark patches in fields; leaving stubbles and not spraying them.

ORGANISATIONS TO SUPPORT

RSPB.

CHANCES OF SURVIVAL IN BRITAIN TO 2050

5/5

I f ever a single animal spoke about the natural crisis facing Britain, it would be the skylark. Its fate speaks of unbearable loss. At the moment, though, there is also hope for it; a hope frighteningly reachable, yet tantalisingly distant.

The skylark is the quintessential farmland bird, and around the management of farms its fortunes lie. Not so long ago (1968–72) it was Britain's most widespread species by area, which, bearing in mind that about 60% of Britain is farmland, is not much of a surprise. It is a common enough bird to enter British phrases such as 'up with the lark'. That very phrase intimately tells of those cold mornings in the early hours' darkness when the farmer's spirits would be lifted by the gorgeous outpourings of the singing lark, a fellow pre-dawn riser. It is a literal riser; it sings in flight, gaining in height, flutter by flutter up to 30m, singing all the while a stream of fast, ecstatic notes that seem as continuous as the flowing of a mountain stream. It sings high, it sings in spirited fashion. Anybody who walks the fields of summer has probably been metaphorically rained upon by its showers of song.

In recent years, however, the airwaves above the fields have started to lose their exuberant soundtrack, as the skylark population has spun into crisis. In farmland, the countrywide population fell by 75% between 1972 and 1996. During the 1990s alone, the number of larks has halved. It has plummeted so much that the traffic light of Conservation Concern has switched to red.

This isn't just a bird disappearing, but a companion. *The Lark Ascending*, written by Ralph Vaughan Williams at the dawn of the First World War, is regularly voted as Britain's favourite piece of classical music. We could be entering into a period where more people are aware of the piece than the bird itself. The music is sublime, but to experience the fresh air and sun, with a skylark singing exultantly above you, is so much more so.

Skylarks have been well studied and the threats to them are clear. The biggest problem for skylarks is probably one that most people have never even heard about. Farmers used to sow their cereal crops in the spring, whereas these days most sow their crops in the autumn, often a month after harvest. Autumn sowing allows the crops a few weeks to grow and to get established before the winter sets in. Once the fair weather arrives, they tend to be taller and denser than spring grown crops. This is good news for the farmer, but the dense sward is a disaster for skylarks and other birds. They simply cannot physically nest there, and if they do use fields of autumn crops, the nests are usually near slightly open places such as tractor tramlines, making the nests vulnerable. As a result, many fewer young skylarks are raised each year.

Autumn sowing is also the death knell for winter stubble, when the harvested crops are left in situ, the ground isn't sprayed with herbicide for months and weeds grow up to provide food for skylarks and many other birds. This valuable resource is lost at a stroke with autumn sowing, where herbicides and pesticides are sprayed into the new crop.

Farmers need to make a living, so it is a bit much to ask them suddenly to switch to spring sowing so that skylark numbers, as well as insect diversity, is improved. However, RSPB researchers at the appropriately named Hope Farm, in Cambridgeshire, discovered in the early 2000s that, if farmers left many small strips (16–24 square metres) of land untilled while sowing their winter crops, then the skylarks would have adequate winter food and space to nest. All they needed to do was to turn off the drill every so often during the sowing process to leave these fallow areas. Areas with these bare patches were found to hold 50% more skylarks. The researchers estimated that, if 20% of arable crops in the UK had 200 skylark plots per square kilometre, the bird's decline could be completely reversed.

Again, nobody was expecting farmers to do this out of pure kindness, so skylark plots (together with leaving stubbles unsprayed and providing fallow land in spring) were added to the government's Entry Level Environment Scheme, a cash incentive available to every farmer in Britain. Economic analyses showed that helping to save skylarks was well rewarded. What was not to like?

Apparently, quite a lot. Up to the present, the incentives haven't been as successful as might be expected and nowhere near enough farmers have taken up the offer. There are issues about the amount of money paid and how it is paid. Skylarks are still declining at their alarming rate.

For many years, Britain's farmers and their representatives have styled themselves as the guardians of the countryside. They claim, sometimes angrily, that they know more in their little finger about how to work the land than any townie. That may be true but, under the present system, agricultural production is denuding the wider countryside. Farmers need and deserve our support. But somehow, things must change, and a revival in skylark numbers would make a good start.

Just recently a trickle of optimism has begun to flow through Britain's parched and fractious agricultural land. Although not all farmers are yet embracing wide-scale change, we might be shifting to an undercurrent of agreement among them. Without sacrificing the bottom line, some are shifting to organic, some are creating cooperatives of interested farmers, and still others wait in the wings for encouragement. A sea-change might be on the way on dry land. We can help by buying organic, and also buying directly from farmers who would like to help the environment. We can write to the National Farmers' Union or other outlets to express our support for environmentally friendly farming. We need to call out the farmers that want to help. The lark's cry may not yet be in vain.

Barn Owl

Tyto alba

FACT FILE

DISTRIBUTION

Widely distributed but localised
across most of Britain and Ireland,
but absent from most Scottish islands.
Present all year.

CURRENT STATUS

Least Concern.

PAST AND CURRENT POPULATIONS

Past unknown, about 4,000 pairs in
1995–97. Current estimated 4,000–
14,000 pairs.

DESCRIPTION OF THE SPECIES

33–39cm long, wingspan 80–95cm.
Looks pale or almost white in flight,
but is intricately patterned with white,
cream, golden-buff. Has white, heart-
shaped face with small black eyes.

DESCRIPTION OF THE THREATS

Agricultural intensification;
fewer rough grasslands;
fewer nest sites owing to decay
or rebuilding on farms; rodenticide
poisoning; collisions with cars.

WHAT WE NEED TO DO

Provide strips of rough grassland;
put up barn owl boxes; adopt a barn
owl; drive at slower speeds.

ORGANISATIONS TO SUPPORT

Barn Owl Trust.

CHANCES OF SURVIVAL
IN BRITAIN TO 2050

5/5

D o you like barn owls? Most people do. In an online ballot for Britain's National Bird, conducted in 2015, the barn owl was voted the second most popular species in Britain, behind the robin. It was obviously the robin. The chances of any bird beating the robin are about the same as the England football team's prospects of beating Germany in a meaningful tournament.

So, the barn owl is popular. It is also stunningly beautiful, mysterious, charismatic and useful. It is also in decline in Britain.

Did you know that there is a small way you can genuinely help barn owls in this country, whoever you are? It's a small change in your driving habits.

The barn owl is a nocturnal predator of small mammals and it has some extraordinary abilities. It has soft feathers which are fitted with fluffy edges to reduce the sound that the owl makes in flight. Although this ensures that a sharp-sensed animal such as a mouse is unlikely to hear the owl coming, the main reason is that, without its own wings making a noise, the owl can hear what is happening around it. All it takes is a rustle and squeak, and the predator can hear its prey. But its party trick is still more extraordinary than acute hearing – its three-dimensional hearing.

Barn owls, like ourselves, have two ears, one on each side of the head. When a noise happens to the side, the sound waves reach one ear before the other, and the minute difference gives us directional hearing in the horizontal place. Unlike us, though, barn owls have non-symmetrical ear openings: the left ear is slightly above the right ear on the side of the head. This means that any sound coming from above or below will reach one ear before the other, conferring directional hearing in the vertical plane. Add the dimensions together and the extraordinary result is that a barn owl can catch prey in total darkness, simply by using its ears. It strikes its prey to an accuracy of one degree.

Worldwide, the barn owl is a highly successful species. So long as there are plenty of small mammals around, and a place to nest – a ledge in a barn, or a nest box is perfect – it will thrive. In this country, it was always likely to have been much more common in the past than now, when barns would sometimes be swarming with rats and mice and there were still plenty of meadows and marginal lands. Nobody ever successfully counted barn owls, so we don't have any reliable figures to compare then to now. Nobody doubts that the species has declined, but the evidence is anecdotal. The current estimate is the wide range of 4,000–14,000 pairs.

So far, the barn owl has not declined far enough to treat it as a crisis, but nevertheless perhaps we should treat its low numbers as such. Barn owls are a prime indicator of the healthy countryside; if there are only 4,000 pairs, that isn't a very impressive figure.

In general, barn owls need 14–47 hectares of rough grassland within reach of a potential nest site, and not many people own that much. However, if you are a farmer, a friend of a farmer or a relative, you can help these birds enormously by allowing strips of rough grassland to run through land. The grassland needs a layer of litter to support the rodents (mainly voles) on which the owls feed. There is a fantastic group called the Barn Owl Trust, which provides all the information you could possibly need.

Assuming there is enough rough grassland in an area, all the owls then need is a good nesting site. In case there is a lack of suitable buildings or trees with holes, you can put up boxes for these birds. The Barn Owl Trust helps to erect boxes all over the country. It is a superb charity which, as usual, needs your money (see page 239). To make it particularly personal, you can adopt an individual barn owl and take part in fundraising. You might even wish to make a barn owl nest box yourself, which directly helps the birds (see page 187).

I mentioned at the start something we can all do to help barn owls. It is an exceptionally environmentally friendly change we can all make. It also saves us money.

The fact is that one of the biggest threats to barn owls is being run over. Road verges sometimes swarm with small mammals, and barn owls naturally hunt by flying over a patch of ground low down and slowly, two factors that make them vulnerable to collisions. If cars went slower on country roads, this would happen less often.

There are a stack of reasons why people should, at the very least, stick to the speed limit: fuel consumption, human safety and wildlife safety, to name but three. But I live in a village with barn owls, and I know that people rarely slow down. But we all could. Next time you're driving on a country road, why not make a mental note to let off the pedal a little? If you're not the driver, why not subtly convey your love for barn owls and their fraught relationship with traffic? A world with slower cars would reflect a better world. And as evidenced in many of the cases in this book, it could happen.

Common Frog

Rana temporaria

--- **FACT FILE** ---

DISTRIBUTION

Throughout the British Isles, other than some northern Scottish islands. Active from February (even January) until October.

CURRENT STATUS

Least Concern, but partially protected.

PAST AND CURRENT POPULATIONS

Unknown, in the millions. Known to be declining in places.

DESCRIPTION OF THE SPECIES

Adult 60–80mm long. Tadpoles are 35mm long and swim in water. Typical frog shape with smooth skin. Has dark patch behind the eye and black dorsal spots. Variable in colour and pattern.

DESCRIPTION OF THE THREATS

Pond draining; general development with more barriers; road casualties; climate change.

WHAT WE NEED TO DO

Promote frogs in gardens by putting in a pond and making a compost heap; eradicate slug pellets; become a toad patroller.

ORGANISATIONS TO SUPPORT

Froglife; Amphibian and Reptile Conservation Trust.

CHANCES OF SURVIVAL IN BRITAIN TO 2050

5/5

Not everybody loves frogs. After all, in the Grimms' fairy tale 'The Frog Prince', the princess has to go through the ultimate ordeal of kissing the rubbery-nosed amphibian before the latter transforms into a handsome prince, so presumably the authors couldn't think of anything else much more dreadful for a girl to do (in an earlier version, she threw the frog against the wall). Today, though, a potentially worse ordeal awaits us. We might have to kiss frogs goodbye.

Frogs are declining in Britain, and so are their rough-skinned relatives, the toads. This decline is mirrored elsewhere in the world; in fact, the extinction of amphibians is one of the most severe biodiversity disasters there is. Globally, about 100 species have become extinct since the 1980s, almost 500 species are Critically Endangered and the rate of extinction is about 200 times the background ('natural') extinction rate. The question is: does anybody care?

We should care. If something so abundant as a frog or toad is disappearing, that is serious. Amphibians are dependent on good water and productive land, and if either is found wanting, they begin to suffer. Amphibian populations are a good test of normality, you might say. They are a reliable early warning system of serious harm ahead.

Although ecologists recognise that frogs are declining sharply, the evidence is mainly anecdotal so far. However, the RSPB's Garden Wildlife Survey indicated a 17% fall between the years 2014 and 2018. This is worrying because gardens are a key habitat for frogs and a very good refuge from development elsewhere, for example on farmland where ponds are being drained. The situation for toads is much more worrying. A study in 2016 suggested that toad populations have dropped by 68% over the last 30 years, at 2.2% per annum. Extrapolate that and they will be gone by 2050. More intense land use, such as housing developments, plus pollution and climate change are all put forward as reasons. About one-third of all the ponds in the UK have been drained in the last 50 years.

One extra problem that amphibians have is that they breed in ponds and wetlands, but spend much time on land, for example under stones and in damp grassland, hedgerows and woodland. So both frogs and toads constantly go hop-about, ranging widely from one place to another, and this means that fragmentation of habitat – cutting access by putting in walls and buildings, or laying roads, for example – means they are vulnerable to being squashed by vehicles and attacked by predators, especially cats, on their travels. Frogs will range about 500m from their breeding ponds, while toads, remarkably, may travel as much as 5km. In the spring and autumn, large numbers of toads, in particular, migrate to breeding or hibernation sites and are slaughtered on the roads. It is estimated that 20 tonnes of toads are squashed every spring and summer on Britain's roads, equivalent to half a million animals.

Despite the gloom, there is much that we, the general public, can do to help frogs and toads, and provide hope for their future. We can do far more, in fact, than you might imagine.

The simple act of putting in a pond in a garden where one is lacking is a huge boost to all kinds of wildlife. Frogs will invariably find new ponds during their nocturnal perambulations. There are far fewer ponds in this country than there used to be, so any addition is a boost. If you are building one, note that to attract breeding frogs it needs to be a couple of metres across, but smaller ponds and wet areas will still attract them to feed and bask. Make sure that there are shallow sections and rocks and stones to help them move around.

You might not have a suitable garden, but if you are daring, you might persuade your school, church (or other faith group), social club or other local outfit with some neglected space to make one – what about your football or cricket club, say? Every single pond is a great boost to wildlife.

That, though, isn't all you can do for amphibians. If you cannot create a pond for lack of space or concerns about infants and toddlers, you can still create a compost heap, which is essentially a fast-food outlet for amphibians, full of the slugs, flies, worms and other invertebrates which they devour. Amphibians often use compost heaps as relatively warm places to hibernate. But even if this is too much, you can also simply create piles of stones, rocks or logs in the garden and both frogs and toads will bask in them, search for food and possibly hibernate.

It should also go without saying that slug pellets are a complete no-no if you want to help amphibians; instead of helping, you'll kill them. Avoid all chemicals and pesticides. Be completely organic (see page 184).

Finally, here is a real left-field way of helping the amphibians in your life. Give up a few nights in the spring and really surprise your friends with what you are getting up to.

As mentioned earlier, in the spring (January–April) toads migrate to the ponds where they hatch. This often means crossing roads at night. Believe it or not, you can sign up to become a toad patroller. On suitable nights, often warm and wet, you will attend a traditional crossing site and literally help the toads across the road! You don't put out a lollipop sign and beckon the amphibians to cross, as at a school crossing. Instead you collect the toads in a bucket and yank them across the highway yourself, something that isn't, by the way, recommended to help children. The process can be laborious and last several hours, and several nights of the spring, and will require some commitment to being outside, getting wet and handling obstreperous, thoroughly ungrateful amphibians.

Let's face it, there aren't many toad patrollers. But in 2019, over 200,000 toads were helped across Britain's roads. Amazing!

Check out the Froglife website for more information.

Slow Worm

Anguis fragilis

FACT FILE

DISTRIBUTION

Most of UK mainland but not Ireland. Localised.

CURRENT STATUS

Priority Species in UK Biodiversity Action Plan.

PAST AND CURRENT POPULATIONS

Unknown. Declining in some areas.

DESCRIPTION OF THE SPECIES

35–40cm long. Very snake-like legless lizard with a shiny, smooth skin. Colour grey-brown (males) or golden-brown (females), often with dark stripe down back.

DESCRIPTION OF THE THREATS

General development; agricultural intensification.

WHAT WE NEED TO DO

Look after its fortunes in gardens, especially by providing compost heap, rocks; don't use slug pellets.

ORGANISATIONS TO SUPPORT

Amphibian and Reptile Conservation Trust.

CHANCES OF SURVIVAL IN BRITAIN TO 2050

5/5

t isn't particularly slow and it isn't a worm. It looks exactly like a small snake, but it isn't one of these, either – after all, it can blink and, when the need arises, can dispense with its tail to help its escape from the clutches of predators. The misunderstood, under-appreciated slow worm is a legless lizard. That isn't a drunk lizard, but one without legs.

The slow worm gets into those places where we would fear to tread, and it eats things that make us shudder – juicy slugs, spiders, maggots, flies, wriggly worms and the like. It has backward-pointing teeth which are particularly good for holding on to slimy and soft prey. It also eats small snails, which doubtless wish that their pursuer did live up to its name.

Slow worms are cold-blooded, requiring external heat to get them moving, and on cold days individuals may not move much at all. They hibernate from October onwards, often in a disused rodent burrow, and sometimes several together. They become active again in March and mate in April to June. They give birth in the late summer to live young. Females can look as fat as pork sausages in their late stages of pregnancy. This isn't entirely surprising, because they can produce clutches of up to 25 young.

This is the sort of animal that forms the unglamorous fabric of our environment. It is common and widespread, although known to be declining. Even more than our other snakes and lizards, it is extremely secretive, usually hiding under rocks or in deep vegetation. This makes it almost impossible to estimate how many slow worms there are, and by how much their populations might be dropping. They aren't faring well in parts of Scotland and the Midlands. There is little doubt that the usual twin curses of farming intensification and rampant development have hurt slow worms, as they have so many other forms of wildlife.

However, the great hope for the slow worm is that it does well in gardens, and here we can help it for all it is worth. The greatest attraction, the one that makes every slow worm leap for joy, is a compost heap. There can be few more wildlife-friendly features, which at the same time are so easy to provide, than compost heaps, and really every single garden should have one, even the smallest.

As far as slow worms are concerned, all you need is a heap; they cannot easily get into a purpose-built composting bin, so you will need to cope with at least one 'messy' feature of the garden. Ideally, you will either need a ready-made wooden frame for a compost heap, or delineate your own with wooden boarding or pallets. Make sure that the heap is on a flat surface where excess water can drain away easily. Regulate what you put in; include grass cuttings, small weeds, prunings, fruit peeling, vegetables and kitchen items such as teabags. Avoid meat and any kind of poo (e.g. from your cat) as this will quickly stink the place out. You might be surprised to discover that it's also a good idea to include scrunched-up paper and a little light cardboard as this can provide air pockets, which help with the breaking down. It is a good idea to turn the heap from time to time with a fork, but be very careful, and avoid doing this in the winter when slow worms will be hibernating blissfully in the natural warmth. Either May or October are safe months to turn the heap.

While the compost heap is the must-have for slow worms, there are also other things you can provide in the garden for them. As mentioned above, they tend not to bask in the open, but they do appreciate basking against something warm: this could be a plant pot, rock or paving-stone, for example. If you can bear to, and you have enough room, lay a piece of corrugated iron on the ground amongst thick grass – this is also slow-worm heaven. These reptiles thrive in a garden with structural diversity, with piles of stones and logs, lots of different vegetation and banks of nettles and brambles, things which most garden lovers dislike. Remember, also, that by being fond of slugs and snails, the slow worm is extremely vulnerable to slug pellets, either by being poisoned or by a lack of food. If you attract these lizards, they should do an excellent job of controlling your slugs and small snails for you.

Britain doesn't have many reptiles, and this is by far the most frequent visitor to our gardens. To be honest, it might not be glamorous and it might easily be overlooked, but you should think of this animal as a badge of honour, a sure sign that you are doing your gardening well. If you don't have your own garden, you can still help with community gardens or volunteer to do practical work in a nature reserve. All of it makes a difference.

Adder

Vipera berus

FACT FILE

DISTRIBUTION

Localised throughout most of the UK, but missing from large parts of middle England and all of Ireland.

CURRENT STATUS

Declining. UK Biodiversity Action Plan Priority Species.

PAST AND CURRENT POPULATIONS

Unknown.

DESCRIPTION OF THE SPECIES

Male 40–55cm long, female 50–70cm. A short, chunky snake with dark zigzag pattern all along its back. Often has an X on its head. Males often have whitish background, females brownish.

DESCRIPTION OF THE THREATS

Fragmented populations; less top-quality habitat; persecution; predation.

WHAT WE NEED TO DO

Protect places where they are; create corridors joining populations; report sightings.

ORGANISATIONS TO SUPPORT

Amphibian and Reptile Conservation Trust.

CHANCES OF SURVIVAL IN BRITAIN TO 2050

4/5

Many people would not mind at all if Britain's only venomous snake were to become extinct. The idea of having any potentially harmful creature in our midst is not popular, especially in our risk-averse society. The irony is that only about 100 people every year end up needing medical attention for adder bites, while 3,500 people every year sustain injuries from dog bites, yet people are far more afraid of the snake than the pet. Adder bites can be harmful, of course, and they can cause a severe reaction, as can a bee or wasp sting. However, since 1876 only 14 people have died in the UK from an adder bite, the last one in 1975. Adders bite dogs quite frequently, but very few dogs succumb either.

The existence of a venomous snake in Britain throws up an intriguing mix of attitudes. What kind of countryside do we want? Do we really want it to be completely safe and bloodless all the time? What kind of a world would that be? Imagine if there were no trees to climb and potentially fall from, thorns to pierce us, thistles to inconvenience our backside, nettles to sting us, wasps to buzz us, spiders to give us the creeps. Life without risk is no life at all. Isn't it great that sometimes the wildlife around us is prepared to bite back? We aren't the masters of everything.

Well, anyway, those who would prefer to have no venomous snakes in our country at all might soon get their way. The adder is in steep decline, so much so that its future could soon be as an animal confined to a limited number of locations, rather than a widespread member of our fauna. Over the last 40 years it has disappeared from much of the Midlands, and is now thought to be gone, or all but extinct, in Greater London, Oxfordshire, Buckinghamshire and Nottinghamshire, to name but a selection. Some estimates suggest a 40% reduction in overall UK distribution.

What is worrying conservationists the most is that many areas seem to support tiny populations that are extremely vulnerable to localised events, such as heath fires. A citizen science survey smartly called 'Make the Adders Count' has been running since 2005. It found that 90% of sites with adders present have only a few animals (ten or fewer observations) and that, on these, almost all the populations were declining. Sites with large populations seem to be doing alright at the moment.

The threats facing adders are considerable. They are among a large number of animals, some featured on other pages, which have declined as agriculture has been more demanding and as more and more corners of the countryside are developed for everything from housing to recreation. The adder also suffers from a few rather more unexpected problems. Pheasants often kill adders by pecking them to death, so adders don't do well in areas with large releases of these game birds. In the country overall, about 57 million pheasants and partridges are released for shooting annually, and some experts fear that this could decimate some adder populations. Buzzards and other raptors, themselves recovering from decades of persecution, include snakes on their menu.

In contrast to grass snakes, which are peripatetic, adders never travel very far, which means that they are poor at colonising new areas and crossing new boundaries, such as roads and other obstructions. They are also fussy about their habitat, preferring dry, open places with low vegetation, such as moors, heathland, chalk downland, woodland edge, sand dunes and hedgerows. This naturally isolates populations, making each one vulnerable and setting in train possible local extinctions.

Recently, it has been shown that adders are extraordinarily reliant on places to spend the winter, known as hibernacula. These are often in disused rabbit holes and ideally close to favourable basking sites, where the adders can warm up in the spring. Typically, many animals share the same hibernaculum, and if there is construction work or heavy earthwork going on, this can bury the adders alive and destroy a whole sub-population. In the past, some conservation measures have caused mass adder deaths, the sort of friendly fire the snakes don't want.

How do we protect adders? We can join in with the excellent work by conservation organisations, such as the Amphibian and Reptile Conservation Trust, which ensure that the snakes are looked after in reserves, farmers and landowners are given adder-friendly advice where required, and fragmented adder populations can be joined. We can try to ensure that dog-walking is controlled on areas where the pets might come into contact with adders. It is also important to submit any sightings we might have of adders to the above Trust.

In the past, the adder used to be routinely killed by the general public, by gamekeepers and landowners. It is now against the law to disturb, let alone kill, an adder, under the Wildlife and Countryside Act 1981, but that doesn't prevent a visceral reaction and temptation to kill any snake found. We need to realise that the small dash of peril in having a venomous snake in our midst is actually a privilege not a curse.

Seahorse

Hippocampus hippocampus and *Hippocampus guttulatus*

FACT FILE

DISTRIBUTION

Shallow seas around British Isles, but commonest in the south and west.

CURRENT STATUS

Protected under the Wildlife and Countryside Act. IUCN: Data Deficient (both species).

PAST AND CURRENT POPULATIONS

Unknown.

DESCRIPTION OF THE SPECIES

Length to 15cm. Fish with well-known upright stance and armour-plated body, remarkably horse-like head, bent forward. Tail long and used for clinging. *H. hippocampus* has shorter snout, less than a third length of head.

H. guttulatus has longer snout, and small spines project out from head and neck, like a blow-dried mane.

DESCRIPTION OF THE THREATS

Any pollution; disturbance of bed of shallow waters, especially seagrass.

WHAT WE NEED TO DO

Careful monitoring of populations; reduce or ban clam dredging and bottom trawling; monitor leisure activities in key areas.

ORGANISATIONS TO SUPPORT

Marine Conservation Society; Seahorse Trust.

CHANCES OF SURVIVAL IN BRITAIN TO 2050

2/5

We might live on an island here in Britain, but few people, it seems, have any idea of the richness of those waters lapping at our shores. Our marine environment, though, is simply sensational. We have some of the world's greatest colonies of seabirds, mainly in Scotland, and some of the finest intertidal habitats (seabed exposed by the tides, including rock pools) on the planet. We have cold-water coral reefs that rival those of the tropics for their vivid colours, if not their extent. We have remarkable kelp forests, seagrass meadows, large windswept tidal estuaries with thousands of shellfish per square metre, and reefs of ancient horse-mussels. Within our waters, the depth of the ocean can reach 5,000m. Our seas are populated by dolphins and whales, including the iconic orca and even, far offshore, the blue whale, the largest animal ever to have lived. In British waters you can find sea turtles and tuna, rays and skates, jellyfish, lobsters, crabs, oysters and mermaids. Okay, maybe not mermaids.

And you can find seahorses. There are only 50 species of these odd-looking fish in the world, and we've got two of them, the spiny seahorse (*Hippocampus guttulatus*) and the short-snouted seahorse (*H. hippocampus*), which both grow to about 15–17cm long. They are, perhaps, the epitome of the fragility of the seabed and its ecosystem. They are rare here, and are declining around the world as they are among the first animals to go when things go wrong in the marine environment.

Seahorses are also, incidentally, very strange. They are among the few fish in the world with an external skeleton, a sort of armour plating to protect them from predators. Unlike most fish, they have a clearly defined neck and their eyes can move independently of each other. They are the slowest-moving fish in the world, which must be frankly embarrassing (one species can only manage 1.5m an hour), and are such useless swimmers that they spend most of their time holding on to seagrass or other solid matter with their prehensile tail to avoid being swept away. They have a remarkably elaborate courtship routine and form long-term pair bonds. Then it is the male that becomes pregnant and looks after the young. The female lays eggs into the male's sac, he self-fertilises them and they develop inside his body.

And what a wonder that they grace our waters. They are commonest in the south, including the Channel Islands, but both species occur in Scotland, Wales and Ireland, too, and the short-snouted seahorse occurs on the Dogger Bank in the North Sea. Both species occur mainly in banks of seagrass. There is a National Seahorse Database for records and, in a fitting tribute to Britain's penchant for spawning miraculously niche organisations, there is a very active Seahorse Trust.

The British marine environment is poorly protected. Remarkably, seahorses were not given legal protection until 2008, thanks to the Seahorse Trust, and very few marine organisms at all are officially protected. Places where seahorses occur, which are invariably shallow waters, are subject to heavy use. In some of the bays where the species occur, pleasure boats destroy seahorse habitat by dragging anchors through the seagrass beds, which should constitute illegal destruction of the habitat, though nothing

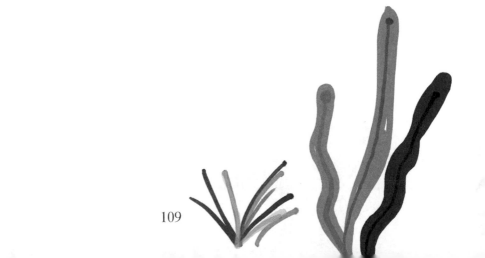

is ever done about it because, by a ridiculous legal loophole, the damage has to be intentional. As if they are going to say: 'Yes, we just wanted to destroy some seahorses.' Such locations are prone to pollution. In one of the best-known sites, Poole Harbour in Dorset, a proposal to drill for oil was only rejected upon judicial review, since it was to be sited in the middle of the core seahorse area; this was a close shave.

There are several deeply destructive practices in the marine environment, few more grotesque than clam fishing. They use a hoover mechanism to suck clams from the seabed, and quite naturally take everything else with them. Both trawlers and clam dredgers have been known to attempt to clean their equipment by dragging it through precious seagrass beds. They are highly destructive and sometimes carried out illegally. Once again, there is little done to stop them.

Our marine environment is extraordinary, but gapingly unprotected. Around the UK there are now 91 Marine Conservation Zones (MCZs), called Marine Protected Areas (MPAs) in Scotland, of which 41 were only declared in spring 2019. They cover less than 1% of our sea area and are a very light form of protection. Extraction, including various forms of fishing, are allowed unless they directly impact upon a ragtag bunch of protected species including seahorses, pink sea fans (see page 161) and breams. There are a few areas in which no catching of anything is allowed, called No Take Zones, but there are vanishingly few of these. Many of the well-established MCZs have no management plan in place.

Seahorses are one of the key species in MCZs, which means that their main habitat, seagrass fields, should also be protected. However, by no means all British seahorses are in MCZs and some of those that are, such as in Studland Bay in Dorset, seem to be decreasing. The future of these wacky fish is far from certain; extinction could happen very quickly.

The existence of seahorses is a symbol of our country's incredible marine heritage; the seahorses themselves are equally a symbol of its vulnerability.

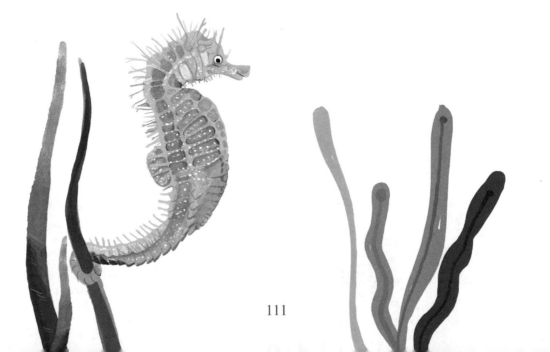

Common Eel

Anguilla anguilla

FACT FILE

DISTRIBUTION

Throughout the British Isles, both in freshwater and estuaries.

CURRENT STATUS

Critically Endangered (UK and worldwide). UK Biodiversity Action Plan species.

PAST AND CURRENT POPULATIONS

Once immense. Unknown, but glass eels arriving in the UK have declined by 95%.

DESCRIPTION OF THE SPECIES

Up to 91cm. A snakelike, long-bodied fish covered in slime. Dorsal fin joins caudal and anal fins. Cryptic and often burying itself in mud or vegetation. Usually dark in colour, paler on the belly.

DESCRIPTION OF THE THREATS

Multiple, including pollution, direct persecution, high predation, parasites, migration hazards, possibly climate change.

WHAT WE NEED TO DO

Careful study and censuses; preserve wetlands; provide migratory pathways; strict regulation of commercial fishing, or halt altogether; report sightings to the Wildlife Trusts.

ORGANISATIONS TO SUPPORT

Zoological Society of London; Wildfowl and Wetlands Trust.

CHANCES OF SURVIVAL IN BRITAIN TO 2050

1/5

Here's a thought to jolt you, especially if you love to eat out. During your life, you might have eaten the flesh of an animal that will be extinct in a few years – not just extinct in Britain, but in the world.

If you have ever eaten eels, you could be in this position. But don't feel guilty, because you are hardly alone. Jellied eels and eel pie have been popular foods since the 18th century, and they were once so common in the River Thames, for example, that eels were a staple food of the poor. The common eel has been eaten all over Europe for centuries. At one time it accounted for 50% of the entire freshwater fish biomass in Europe.

Incredibly, though, the common eel is now one of the very few British animals classed by the International Union for the Conservation of Nature (IUCN) as Critically Endangered worldwide. That is because, over the last 40 years, the number of 'glass eels' (see below) arriving in Europe in the spring has dropped by a deeply alarming 95%.

The eel might once have been common, but it has always been mysterious and poorly understood. And no wonder; its life cycle is extraordinary. An eel's life begins in saltwater, as an egg laid by a mature 'silver' eel in the Sargasso Sea in the North Atlantic, off the coast of the USA. It hatches into a leaf-like larva (a 'leptocephalus'), which joins the plankton drifting north-eastward on the Gulf Stream. After a 6,000km journey lasting two years or more, it reaches European waters and develops into an intermediary finger-length stage known as a 'glass eel', with an almost transparent body. Most then follow their instincts upriver, in the same way as a salmon does, and they darken, becoming known as 'elvers'. They find their way into rivers, ditches and lakes, where they remain, slowly growing, for up to 20 years, by which time the snake-like females may reach 1m in length and be as wide as a human arm. During this phase they are greenish on the back and pale yellow on the belly and are appropriately known as 'yellow eels'. Eventually they grow darker, with a silver belly, reaching sexual maturity as 'silver eels'. This is the cue for them to return to the sea, where they grow larger eyes to cope with the dark depths. Amazingly, their gut dissolves and they no longer feed at all. Progressing at steady pace, they migrate to the Sargasso Sea, spawn and die.

In this turbulent life history of many parts, you can easily imagine that a lot can go wrong. For example, only about 1 in 500 leptocephalus larvae are thought to reach Europe. The migration of glass eels and elvers upriver in spring is also fraught with difficulty, especially with many barriers put up by human beings. Remarkably, both elvers and silver eels, the latter of which migrate back down to the sea in autumn, are capable of slithering over grass and dry ground, and can even climb up walls if they have enough purchase. But hydroelectric schemes, weirs and dams add barriers to their already difficult journey.

We still don't know much about eel migration. We don't know how the silver eels find their way back to the Sargasso Sea, although a sense of the earth's magnetic field has been suggested. We know virtually nothing about their lives as silver eels in the ocean depths.

So, the common eel's precipitous crash in population is, in common with much eel biology, something of a mystery. At the moment, the small number of silver eels reaching Europe is causing the most concern. It is possible that climate change may be shifting the direction of the Gulf Stream. The marine environment is awash with

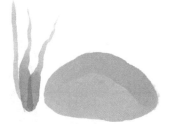

pollution and pesticides, litter and plastic, and eels also suffer from parasitic infections. There is a nematode called *Anguillicola crassus* which causes internal physiological damage, including to the swim-bladder, and infestation might inhibit the silver eels from reaching their spawning grounds. This nematode (a type of flatworm) is not native to Europe but was introduced with Japanese eels, imported for aquaculture in the 1980s.

As mentioned above, the eel's life journey, with its many stages, offers a variety of different threats along the way. Elvers and yellow eels suffer from high predation by cormorants and herons, possibly exacerbated by human activity. All eel stages in Europe are fished by people for commercial and recreational purposes, which is perhaps surprising for a Critically Endangered animal. Some eels are illegally exported to other parts of the world.

It is extremely difficult to be optimistic about the fate of the once-abundant eel. Very few of its major problems are fully understood, let alone in a position to be alleviated. However, that doesn't mean we shouldn't try.

And here conservationists and researchers are doing their best. For example, take the issue that some paths taken upstream by glass eels are known to be blocked by human artefacts. What can we do? In some circumstances, we can literally fetch the eels manually from one side and deposit them on the other. In others, we can build shortcuts for the fish that cut past manmade structures. In one nature reserve in south-west England, a tunnel connects the wetland to an estuary, but at low tides the access point is too high for eels. The solution is to connect an 'eel pass', a plastic gutter with bristles inside that help the glass eels to crawl in. All over Britain and Europe there are projects like this. They need supporting with donations and volunteering.

Scientists are also doing all they can to fill in the many gaps about eel behaviour and migration, including tagging the animals. You might be surprised that you can be involved in citizen science projects to help monitor eels. One such is run by the Zoological Society of London. It is also worth having a look at the website of the Rivers Trust which often runs local eel projects.

You can help the eel by reporting any sightings you might have to the Wildlife Trusts using this email: sightings@wwt.org.uk. You can also tag the Wildlife Trusts in Facebook, Instagram or Twitter posts. It might not seem much help, but all contributions to eel research are vital.

Basking Shark

Cetorhinus maximus

FACT FILE

DISTRIBUTION

Can be seen off any coast, but much commoner in the west, including Cornwall, the Isle of Man and the west of Scotland. June to September.

CURRENT STATUS

Globally Endangered. Protected by law.

PAST AND CURRENT POPULATIONS

Past unknown. Estimated 985 off west Scotland 2010; perhaps 19,100 all Scotland and Ireland.

DESCRIPTION OF THE SPECIES

To 12m, more often 9m. Huge, slow moving fish with long snout, enormous mouth, and five gill-slits encircle body.

DESCRIPTION OF THE THREATS

Formerly from direct persecution for its liver and fins. Very slow reproductive rate makes it vulnerable.

WHAT WE NEED TO DO

Look after marine habitats; avoid collisions with craft; stop any illegal poaching; collect observations.

ORGANISATIONS TO SUPPORT

Shark Trust.

CHANCES OF SURVIVAL IN BRITAIN TO 2050

3/5

Every summer the tabloid newspapers publish photographs of triangular fins sticking out of the water close to a holidaymaker. The headlines scream about giant sharks 'invading' British waters. Be afraid, be very afraid.

Well, there is cause for alarm, but only to plankton. The fins belong to a gentle giant that is less dangerous to humans than a wasp. It is the basking shark, a monster that can grow up to 12m in length, although it rarely reaches more than 9m long in Britain, still pretty big. We should be proud and thrilled to have the basking shark in our waters, because it is the second largest fish in the world, behind the whale shark of tropical seas.

If you wish to be cynical, these tabloid headlines are not only sensational and alarmist, they are also brazenly false. The problem is that sharks generally have a reputation for being dangerous to humans that is vastly out of proportion to the actual threat that they pose. Do you know how many people have been killed by shark attacks in British waters? Zero, unless you count a very dodgy account from the 1930s, when three people were drowned after their boat was allegedly capsized by a basking shark. A few anglers have been bitten when trying to land sharks they have caught, but in court that's known as self-defence. The conclusion is that sharks in reality provide no threat to humans in our waters.

You are very fortunate if you see one. The best chance is in the late summer, when basking sharks move into shallow waters off some parts of Britain (Cornwall, the Isle of Man, west Scotland) and can be seen at the surface on calm days, fins, tail and snout protruding. They appear to 'bask' in the sun, but in reality they are simply swimming slowly forward, allowing the water to enter their mouths so that they can filter out the zooplankton. This extraordinarily passive style of feeding is very unusual. There are only three species of filter-feeding sharks in the world and the other two, the whale shark and the megamouth shark, both have ways of pumping water through their bodies. This method only works when there is a good density of food in the water (for example 1,700 copepods per cubic metre), so basking sharks spend their lives travelling between the best feeding grounds. An individual shark will travel thousands of kilometres a year, spending the winter in deeper water; so you can see what a privileged encounter it always is with this enormous and very mysterious creature.

Although it is found in many parts of the world in cooler waters, the basking shark is officially classified as globally Endangered. It has faced some threats similar to those of whales: over-exploitation by humans, a population slump and, in some areas such as Europe, a painfully slow recovery. In our waters it still faces some threats to its survival.

There is no doubt that, until the mid-1940s, the basking shark was still common worldwide. Since then, however, it is thought that numbers have declined by anywhere between 50% and 79%. Needless to say, this has been brought about by human activity. Up until recently, the basking shark was targeted in many ways for its meat, fins, cartilage and liver oil. As a large, slow-swimming fish it was often caught by harpoon and by net as food. The cartilage is still valued in Chinese and Japanese folk medicine, and the fins, in particular, have been used in shark-fin soup. In an analogy to the tragic trade in rhino horn, the fins and cartilage have for centuries been believed to have aphrodisiac properties. It's nonsense, of course, but a few years ago a single, large basking shark fin could fetch $57,000. Unfortunately, the best fins often come from the largest specimens, usually breeding-age females, which may take a couple of decades to reach maturity.

These days commercial fishing for basking sharks has been banned in many parts of the world, including the UK and EU. This is all very well, but the previous damage wrought by over-exploitation has repercussions for the present. The basking shark's biology makes it dangerously vulnerable. It is slow to mature and only produces a small number of young. Killing any male basking shark that is less than 12 years old, and any female under 20, wipes out their lifetime reproductive output; even at 20, a female will have barely begun reproducing. Nobody knows how long pregnancy lasts, although it is estimated at 14 months. The only pregnant female ever caught was carrying six pups, which is not a large number. The widespread killing in the past will still take decades to heal – the International Union for the Conservation of Nature suggests that it could be hundreds of years.

Even today in British waters, basking sharks aren't safe. They have a habit of ignoring vessels, which means that collisions happen, causing injuries and death. In addition, these large fish get caught up in lines for lobster pots. They are also taken as bycatch, although it is compulsory to return any survivors to the sea. In the current state each small accident, especially to a breeding-age adult, can have wide ramifications to local populations.

As members of the public, we rarely encounter basking sharks, but we can help them. We can donate to the Shark Trust, sponsor an individual shark, report any stranded individuals or those being harassed, and go on responsibly run boat trips to see them for ourselves. It is also important to report any sightings of this poorly understood animal, especially if we have photographs that might enable an individual to be recognised.

If you are lucky enough to see one, though, just don't report it to the papers.

The Shark Trust website has more information on conservation of basking sharks.

White-clawed Crayfish

Austropotamobius pallipes

FACT FILE

DISTRIBUTION

Crystal-clear hard waters along rivers in England and Wales up to Scottish borders.

CURRENT STATUS

Endangered (IUCN and UK). Protected by law. UK Biodiversity Action Plan species.

PAST AND CURRENT POPULATIONS

Unknown but everywhere in severe decline, for example by 95% in Thames area, 95% Hampshire, 100% Sussex, 31% south-west England.

DESCRIPTION OF THE SPECIES

10cm long. Looks like a brown lobster in freshwater, with the usual pincers. Claws don't look white.

DESCRIPTION OF THE THREATS

Introduced alien crayfish, mainly signal crayfish which bring crayfish plague.

WHAT WE NEED TO DO

Protect areas with native crayfish and try to keep non-native crayfish and plague away; reintroduce into cleared areas.

ORGANISATIONS TO SUPPORT

Rivers Trust; Wildlife Trusts.

CHANCES OF SURVIVAL IN BRITAIN TO 2050

1/5

It is highly unlikely that you have ever woken up in the middle of the night, sweating and thinking: 'What is going to happen to the white-clawed crayfish?' It's probably best that you haven't, because the future looks extremely bleak for our only native 'freshwater lobster'. It could be on the way to extinction, sweat or no sweat.

Perhaps, though, you are the sort of person for whom the plight of the red squirrel genuinely does upset you. If so, you might be interested to know that the story of the white-clawed crayfish and that of the red squirrel are extraordinarily similar. The crayfish's fate mirrors that of the squirrel underwater. You might like to compare the squirrel's story on pages 26–31.

There was a time, not so long ago, when the white-clawed crayfish was common over much of the country, occurring in clean, shallow, well-oxygenated rivers and other waterways, up as far as the Scottish borders. It was so familiar, indeed, that it was widely eaten. Samuel Pepys mentioned eating 'trouts, eels and crayfish' at Hungerford in 1688, and parties would often be held to enjoy their delicious flesh. In autumn, when the water was warm, you could catch them at their most sluggish. As with marine lobsters, the flesh in the claws is the best part.

Crayfish don't have particularly pleasant habits. They are scavengers on dead flesh on the riverbed and also voracious predators, feeding mainly at night. They catch snails, insect larvae and occasional fish, which they hold or crush with their powerful pincers and transfer to the jaws for slow grinding down. They mate in the autumn and store the eggs on the bristles of their appendages; when these hatch they are a mini-version of the adults and will often cannibalise each other, especially when moulting into a new exoskeleton, a time when they are very vulnerable.

White-clawed crayfish might be insalubrious, but at least they are ours, born and bred Brits. What happened in the 1980s was quite frankly scandalous and should never ever have been allowed.

What did happen was that the government of the day encouraged people to set up crayfish farms, and even provided money for start-ups. Whilst this might have been fine had the native crayfish been bred, it wasn't because most of these farms were instead stocked with a different species of crayfish. The signal crayfish comes from North America. It is easier to farm than our white-clawed crayfish and is larger and meatier. So, farms up and down the country were stocked with the Americans.

Well, with hindsight it was obvious what would happen. There were mass breakouts. Soon signal crayfish began to appear in many British rivers.

Is this sounding familiar yet? The parallels with the Anglo-American squirrel squabble are uncanny.

It is hard to believe, but people knew in the 1980s that the signal crayfish posed an insidious threat to the native crayfish by carrying a fungal disease. While the American species could usually shake it off, it was invariably fatal to the white-clawed crayfish.

Once infected, the unfortunate beasts would leave the water, even in the middle of the day, wander about shakily, keel over with their legs in the air and expire. The inevitable happened. Signal crayfish brought the plague to our wetlands. White-clawed crayfish died off and they were replaced by their enemies. This has happened all over the country.

Time and again, the introduction of an alien species occurs and has catastrophic consequences. The crayfish saga could have been avoided, but the rule-makers fouled up.

The white-clawed crayfish has been described as the UK's 'black rhino'. Unless extensive conservation efforts are directed in its favour, it will certainly be wiped out. In recent years, Scottish Natural Heritage spent £100,000 trying to remove signal crayfish in the Scottish Borders by poisoning them or fishing them out, but it proved to be a costly and futile exercise – a signal failure, you might say.

White-clawed crayfish are now confined to a few isolated waterways. Not only is there a risk of introduced crayfish finding their way to these sites, but the fungal disease carrying the crayfish plague easily contaminates the water and could be brought in accidentally.

Remember that this was all preventable. Conservationists and scientists have known for decades that introducing foreign species is a bad idea, yet it was allowed to happen in the case of signal crayfish. The government allowed the American to be introduced for quite deliberate economic reasons, hoping to start a lucrative export trade to Europe. It is yet another example of how, in the echelons of power, bad ideas can flourish on the promise of short-term economic gain.

What can be done now? Conservation efforts have concentrated on protecting the last sites where there are good populations of white-clawed crayfish. Other rivers can then be cleared of signal crayfish and, after there is no longer any crayfish plague remaining, the native crayfish can then be reintroduced.

There is also one, rather unusual, way that people can help. Some companies have sprung up that catch signal crayfish and offer them for food. Some claim that they can help white-clawed crayfish if enough people take a liking to the interlopers.

In truth, it's probably too late. However, crayfish are delicious, and you at least can eat the British-caught signal crayfish in the faint hope that you are doing some good!

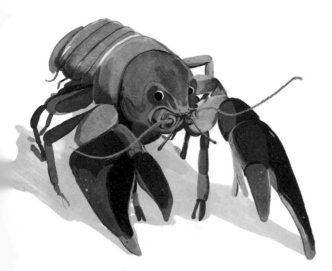

Large Blue

Phengaris arion

--- **FACT FILE** ---

DISTRIBUTION

Well-drained unimproved grassland, of chalk, in Cornwall, Devon, Somerset, Gloucestershire. Flies late June and throughout July.

CURRENT STATUS

Critically Endangered (UK). Near Threatened (IUCN). Endangered (Europe). Priority Biodiversity Action Plan species. Fully protected.

PAST AND CURRENT POPULATIONS

Small then zero in 1979. Reintroduced 1983/4 and now a few thousand.

DESCRIPTION OF THE SPECIES

Wingspan male 38—48mm, female 42—52mm. Vivid blue upperside with black edges and a half-ring of black spots on forewing.

DESCRIPTION OF THE THREATS

Formerly collecting; reduction in chalk down habitats.

WHAT WE NEED TO DO

Continue reintroducing to old haunts and keep careful watch on current population.

ORGANISATIONS TO SUPPORT

Butterfly Conservation; National Trust.

CHANCES OF SURVIVAL IN BRITAIN TO 2050

3/5

Sometimes, in conservation, everything feels so overwhelming that the actions of just one or two people would seem to be completely futile. The case of the large blue, and the foresight of Professor Jeremy Thomas and David Simcox, proves that such a negative conclusion is untrue. The right people, at the right time, can make an astonishing difference.

The large blue butterfly was always rare in Britain, confined to a few sunny slopes across southern England. Back in the days of the Victorian craze for butterfly collecting, that made it vulnerable; people would go to the remaining colonies and virtually clear them out. This, combined with a steady reduction of its favoured habitat of close-cropped, south-facing chalky slopes, meant that the rare large blue became the very rare large blue and, after a couple of wet and unfavourable British summers, the extinct large blue in 1979.

Thomas and Simcox were among many who decided that this would not be the end of the story. These two scientists, however, were well positioned to find out crucial details about how the butterfly might be reintroduced. What might it need to survive? Was there anything missing in our knowledge of the large blue that might make a critical difference?

Much was already known about the butterfly and, in some ways, it was not entirely surprising that the large blue was rare: it was a butterfly with extraordinarily exacting requirements, a total diva in the ecological sense.

Most butterflies lay their eggs on a food plant, the eggs hatch, the caterpillar eats the leaves of the plant, they turn into pupa and, in time, emerge as adult butterflies – thank you very much, food plant. However, butterfly enthusiasts had tried rearing large blues in the past by duly providing them with the plant on which they lay their eggs, wild thyme. It didn't work. Eventually, scientists found out the reason why. Once the eggs hatch, the caterpillar begins its new life as a herbivore, but turns carnivorous. It drops off the thyme leaves and sends out chemical signals that mimic those of ants. The ants, fooled into thinking that the caterpillar is one of their own, retrieve the caterpillar and bring it into their nest, and here the large blue caterpillar sets about returning the favour by eating the ants' grubs. It keeps on beguiling its guests with happy chemical messages, and will even rubs its segments together and effectively sing a happy song. Its tummy full of its hosts' babies, it contentedly pupates, and the large blue adult hatches out the following summer.

One of the crucial contributions made by our human heroes in the large blue story was that they were able to determine that only one ant species becomes an effective host for the large blue, a black ant called *Myrmica sabuleti*. Once they knew that and the rest of the strange life-history, they argued that it should be possible to reintroduce the large blue into areas with good populations of the host, ready and willing to be duped.

The story is proverbial. They found out that Swedish large blues were a genetic match for ours. They then asked the Swedes to lend us some larvae, which the Scandinavians were happy to do. They then had to obtain from government three licences, one to import the larvae, one to release them into the wild and one to monitor how they were getting on. Nobody, as far as I am aware, ever approached the ants' representatives to see what they thought of this. It is probably a good thing that they never raised an objection.

So, in the summer of 1983, a campervan full of large blue larvae made its way to the potential new home, a former haunt of the species on Dartmoor. The first introductions were successful, so the trial was widened to include nine further sites in the Cotswolds, Somerset and Cornwall. By 2016 over 10,000 large blues were flying over the chalky slopes of Somerset and Gloucestershire, even at the very well-known public site of Collard Hill in Somerset, a site owned by the National Trust. Fashions have changed, and even at a well-known site, the deprivations wrought by butterfly collectors are much reduced.

In 2019, the largest reintroduction of the large blue yet has been made into Rodborough Common, in Gloucestershire, where the last butterflies flew more than 150 years ago; 750 butterflies were counted in 2020.

Ironically, and astonishingly, there are now more large blues in Britain than anywhere else in the world. This globally threatened butterfly is commoner here than in its parent country, Sweden.

While it naturally took teams of professionals and volunteers to do the groundwork in reintroducing the large blue over many years – and everybody involved should take their share of congratulations, including Butterfly Conservation, the National Trust and the Back from the Brink Partnership – the fact is that the enquiring minds and foresight of just one or two people enabled this to happen. Thomas and Simcox made the crucial discovery in identifying the requirements of the butterfly, and their tenacity ensured that the reintroduction was eventually given the green light. The large blue project is now thought to be the most successful reintroduction of an insect anywhere in the world.

Sometimes, a handful of like minds and a lot of imagination can change the world for the better.

Small Tortoiseshell

Aglais urticae

FACT FILE

DISTRIBUTION

Throughout the UK, although scarcer towards the north. Flies from March to November.

CURRENT STATUS

Least Concern, but declining.

PAST AND CURRENT POPULATIONS

Unknown, but apparent 73% decline recently.

DESCRIPTION OF THE SPECIES

Adult is predominantly orange with both wings bordered by thread of blue beads. Leading edge of forewing stripy. At rest easy to overlook, like a dead leaf, dark inner and pale outer half of wings. Sexes alike. Caterpillars are yellow and black, with hairs, but conspicuously cluster together in webs on nettles.

DESCRIPTION OF THE THREATS

Uncertain. Some parasite infections; possibly fewer hibernation sites.

WHAT WE NEED TO DO

Provide good range of flowers, including nettles.

ORGANISATIONS TO SUPPORT

Butterfly Conservation; RHS.

CHANCES OF SURVIVAL IN BRITAIN TO 2050

5/5

Butterflies are delight in animate form. Decorated with dazzling colours, with paper-thin wings, lacking any stings or physical nuisance and blowing in on the zephyrs of summer, these insects are a joy. Common around gardens and at ease with human habitation, they live among us and, as such, are often the catalyst for a child's wonder about the natural world. Their strange metamorphosis, from egg to larva to pupa and a butterfly, is another conduit into the study of nature, and a metaphor for life too.

Even the most hard-hearted non-conservationist, a person who might think newts are an evil designed by nature to frustrate economic development, would notice if butterflies were to disappear, or at least be sad that they were declining. No soul is untouched by the passing of beauty.

The truth is, though, that butterflies are declining. *The State of Britain's Butterflies*, produced by the charity Butterfly Conservation in 2015 (the next one is imminent), records an alarming drop of abundance and distribution across our 60 or so species. 70%

of all our species are less widespread than they were in 1976, and 57% of our species are less abundant. These figures relate both to habitat-specific species and, more worryingly, what are known as 'wider-countryside species', those which can occur almost anywhere.

The small tortoiseshell is one of our commonest and most widespread butterflies. It has just about the simplest needs you can imagine – flowers for its nectar food and nettles on which to lay its eggs. So, if this easy-to-please animal is dropping in numbers, we ought to be concerned. And it is; it is undergoing a long-term decline, a drop in abundance of 73%. It has always been a butterfly of fluctuating fortunes, but in recent years its overall graph is generally down. It is fair to assume that it doesn't just look like a red flag, it is a red flag. In the summer of 2018, the small tortoiseshell suffered its worst ever summer in the annual Big Butterfly Count, also run by Butterfly Conservation. If this is the shape of things to come, we must sit up and take notice.

Nobody yet knows for sure why the small tortoiseshell has become less abundant, or whether the trend will continue. One reason, though, appears to be the depredations of a parasite, a fly called *Sturmia bella*, which lays its eggs on nettles. The caterpillars of the butterfly ingest these eggs and they hatch out inside the unfortunate animal's body, eat it from the inside and eventually emerge from the dead chrysalis, like an insect version of the film *Alien*. The flies were unknown in Britain before 1999 and it is likely that climate change has played a part.

Another problem for small tortoiseshells is that there might be fewer places to hibernate. It is one of the very few British butterflies to spend the winter in the adult state. One of their favourite places is the great British household. These days, however, houses are so well (and stiflingly) heated that they are simply too warm for the hibernating butterflies. They need a consistently cool, but not freezing, location, such as a garden shed or older, less efficiently heated buildings such as churches. They also use caves and hollow trees.

Whether or not we can help the small tortoiseshell is anybody's guess; it is highly unlikely to die out in Britain, not least because many thousands migrate here from

southern Europe every summer anyway. What we can do, though, is what we do for every garden butterfly, which is to provide lots of nectar-rich flowers for them to feed on. In the case of small tortoiseshells, we should also leave a nettle patch in sunlight where they can lay their eggs.

Providing suitable flowers can start with buddleia, perhaps the most reliable and beautiful shrub you can possibly grow for butterflies, which originates from China. However, be careful because some buddleias are much better than others; the old trick of visiting a garden centre on a hot day and buying only what you see the wild 'customers' feeding on is a smart policy. Interestingly, buddleia is an introduced plant and can be invasive. Frequently, animal and plant introductions are a disaster for the British countryside, but for buddleia, at least in the garden and urban environment, we must hold our noses and set aside condemnation.

Butterflies such as tortoiseshells, which hibernate here as adults, need special treatment in the garden because they can be seen very late in the year, when many other butterflies are over, so remember to plant some late-flowering blooms such as asters. Ivy, which flowers in autumn, is not much loved by gardeners but is a fantastic all-round source of food for many garden animals. Verbena, marjoram and lavender are three other excellent flowers.

Butterflies are easy to attract and look after, so what's not to like? In many ways, they are the flying blooms of the garden, giving as much joy as the plants themselves.

Garden Tiger

Arctia caja

FACT FILE

DISTRIBUTION

Throughout the British Isles.
Flies in July and August.

CURRENT STATUS

Least Concern worldwide, Near
Threatened in UK. Protected in the UK
under the Biodiversity Action Plan.

PAST AND CURRENT POPULATIONS

Unknown, but perhaps now 10% of
what it once was prior to the 1960s.

DESCRIPTION OF THE SPECIES

Forewing 2.8–3.7cm. Chunky-bodied
moth with brilliantly coloured wings,
variably white, brown or black. Famous
caterpillar is 'woolly bear', black and
ginger with long hairs.

DESCRIPTION OF THE THREATS

Hard to say. Perhaps partly climate
change. Far more pollution; fewer
flowers in the countryside.

WHAT WE NEED TO DO

Monitor populations; maintain varied
array of plants in the garden.

ORGANISATIONS TO SUPPORT

Butterfly Conservation.

CHANCES OF SURVIVAL
IN BRITAIN TO 2050

4/5

Looking at the picture, you might be thinking that the garden tiger is a butterfly. It isn't. It's a moth. Moths are the great secret of the garden. They are the hidden jewels of our herbaceous borders, trees and shrubs. In every garden are dozens of species, of every pattern and hue, waiting to be discovered and appreciated. On a single night in June even an average suburban garden will probably be visited by more than a hundred species.

The garden tiger is a particularly gaudy night-flying moth, but many other species are spectacular in their own way. There are pink ones, yellow ones, pearly-white ones, green ones and every shade of brown you can imagine. There are chunky ones, butterfly-like ones and hawk-moths, which are huge, turbo-charged species which often have 'eyes' and other markings to scare potential predators. If you've never tapped into the delicious diversity of moths, you are missing a treat.

One of the unexpected pleasures of 'mothing' is learning their names. There is a mother-of-pearl, a Brussels lace, a rosy footman, a Chinese character, a heart and dart, a burnished brass and a lesser broad-bordered yellow underwing, and hundreds of others. In theory you could find yourself admiring an early grey and an old lady, while sipping Earl Grey tea with an old lady (though sadly the moths fly at different times). These wonderful names imbue 'mothing' culture with a whimsy that sits well with delighting in these mysterious summer-night creatures.

The lives of moths are short but amazing. Some are cannibalistic in their caterpillar form. Adult moths, such as the amazing ruby tiger, can sometimes jam the echolocation signals of bats, their main enemies, to avoid being eaten. Moths migrate, sometimes

for enormous distances; there is evidence that some species, such as the large yellow underwing, can navigate by the stars. Some male moths hatch from their pupal stage and never eat anything again, devoting themselves simply to satisfying their urge to mate. Many species only live in the adult form for a couple of weeks. Moths often disperse to great heights, rising on summer-night zephyrs into a night sky far above our experience and imagination. We cannot easily imagine what their lives might be like.

From this you will realise that there is a lot more to moths that the fluttering, flailing creature which, lost in the sanitised environment of the indoors, flies helplessly at the electric lights. Equally, despite the fact that some people are irrationally afraid of their fluttering, moths are about as harmless as the pillow you sleep upon. Oh yes, there are clothes moths, but only a couple of species out of 2500, and a few species are pests. But overall, moths are not only wonderful, but largely beneficial.

The garden tiger is a good symbol for moth-dom from a conservation perspective, because it, like many other species, has undergone dramatic declines in population in recent years. This species, which has the well-known 'woolly bear' caterpillar, is thought to have fallen in population by 92% since 1968 – one of the steepest falls known for any British animal. It is still common, but clearly in severe retreat. Recent counts have suggested that the overall population of all moths in this country is down 28% since 1968, while in southern England the figure is closer to 40%. 60 species of moths became extinct in the 20th century, although equally quite a few new species have also been established, probably because of climatic changes.

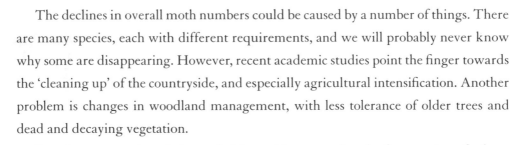

The declines in overall moth numbers could be caused by a number of things. There are many species, each with different requirements, and we will probably never know why some are disappearing. However, recent academic studies point the finger towards the 'cleaning up' of the countryside, and especially agricultural intensification. Another problem is changes in woodland management, with less tolerance of older trees and dead and decaying vegetation.

So, what can we do to help moths? I would suggest that the first step is to find out about them. Attend a 'moth-trapping' session, of which many are run by The Wildlife Trusts, Butterfly Conservation and many wildlife reserves during the summer. If watching a moth-trap being opened doesn't blow you away and make you a fan of moths, nothing will. Such events are also perfect for children, most of whom will adore seeing the shapes and colours and appreciate having some moths on their hand. Moths are brilliant educational tools to fire young conservationists.

Secondly, you can help moths in your gardens (if you have one) and neighbourhood. Most of the things you can do to help moths are the same as those that help butterflies and, indeed, most other wildlife. Grow a wide variety of flowers and shrubs, especially those that provide nectar. Particular favourites of moths include honeysuckle, night-scented stock, jasmine and tobacco-plant. Don't use pesticides, leave a wild patch somewhere in a corner, and allow a modicum of mess. Not cutting back seed heads that have died, and allowing some dead leaves to pile up, will also provide habitat for moths and other insects.

Thirdly, why not join the National Moth Monitoring Scheme, which is run by Butterfly Conservation and has been going since 2007? It is a good way to learn your moths and contribute to our knowledge about these wondrous insects. You can do this even if you don't have a garden, since moths can easily be attracted to lights through any window.

Shrill Carder Bee

Bombus sylvarum

FACT FILE

DISTRIBUTION

Just seven counties: Kent, Essex, Somerset, Wiltshire, Gwent, Glamorgan and Pembrokeshire. Flies from May to September.

CURRENT STATUS

Endangered. Priority Species under post-2010 Biodiversity Framework.

PAST AND CURRENT POPULATIONS

Unknown, but its range has shrunk to a tiny percentage of what it was 100 years ago.

DESCRIPTION OF THE SPECIES

A distinctively small bumblebee just 13mm long (queen), 9mm long (worker). Grey-haired, single black band across the thorax, two dark bands on the abdomen, and a pale orange tip to the abdomen. Makes a high-pitched buzzing, hence the name.

DESCRIPTION OF THE THREATS

The intensification of farming and of grazing regimes; loss of flower-rich grassland.

WHAT WE NEED TO DO

Where the bee still occurs, establish new wildflower grasslands or pollen and nectar margins and leave them flowering through the summer into late September. This is a late emerging bee, so suitable grasslands will need to be cut later in the year than other meadows.

ORGANISATIONS TO SUPPORT

Bumblebee Conservation Trust.

CHANCES OF SURVIVAL IN BRITAIN TO 2050

1/5

Remember that parental dread about the 'birds and the bees' talk? It's changed in recent years. Once it was all about the awkward subject of procreation; now it's all about an equally awkward subject – the decline of so much of our wildlife. And out there the bees, sad to say, are hardly buzzing.

Take the case of the shrill carder bee, one of more than 270 bee species in this country. It was once found throughout England and Wales and up to southern Scotland, but last century it underwent a crash in population and now only remains in seven areas in south Wales, Somerset/Wiltshire, and the Thames Estuary, and is scarce in all of them.

It is perfectly possible that we could lose it altogether. It is a bumblebee, and each nest of 70–80 workers requires an extensive area of flower-rich grassland to survive, a habitat which is vanishing fast. It is something of a fussy bee, with its own pernickety needs, but that makes it essential that we somehow manage to keep it here. Why? Because when there is a trend of decline among a group of animals, the first to go are the fussy ones.

The plight of the shrill carder bee is the thin end of a monumental wedge that, believe it or not, threatens humanity. We need bees, but worldwide bees aren't doing well. Many countries are reporting reductions in the number of honeybees and in the UK, we lost 53% of managed honeybee colonies between 1985 and 2005. We have lost 25 species in the last hundred years or so. Bee diversity has declined in 52% of English landscapes. That could be related to the enormous changes in the countryside over the years, with its wholesale losses of meadows (we have lost 97% since the 1930s) and other habitats and, especially, the large-scale and long-term use of pesticides. One in ten European bee species are threatened with extinction. A recent scientific study concluded that, worldwide, the global mass of insects is reducing by 2.5% a year.

Any reduction in bee numbers is a serious matter because of their extreme importance as pollinators. Bees and other insects are responsible for pollinating 78% of all temperate wildflowers throughout the world, and for at least 20 different UK crops. Some £510 million of crop sales value was generated by pollinators in 2009, and the cost of replacing them is estimated at £1.8 billion a year in labour and pollen. A massive loss of bees and other insect life isn't just an economic matter. Insects are the bedrock of many of our ecosystems, which could collapse with desperate consequences for humanity.

As mentioned above, one big issue for bees that must be addressed is the widespread use of pesticides in farming and gardens. In particular, a class of chemicals known as neonicotinoids have major effects on these insects, reducing their breeding success, overall health, disease resistance, foraging efficiency and homing. That is quite a lot of negatives, yet incredibly, not only are these pesticides legally applied, the companies that produce them continue to protest that they aren't as destructive as claimed. These companies are one of the evils of the age; they are the equivalent of tobacco companies to humans, creating a product they know is dangerously destructive to the natural world.

But how can we help bees? We can start in our gardens. Never underestimate how much good you can do in your own backyard. And start by resolving never to use pesticides or weed killers.

We don't need our gardens to be so tidy as we seem to these days. We can allow some weeds that are good for bees. If we allow the grass on our lawns to grow just to 8–10cm, it allows wonderful bee-friendly flowers to grow such as clovers, daisies, self-heal and buttercups. These are glorious in their own right if you are prepared to tolerate them. They don't make the lawn look rank and unduly messy.

Better still, if you have enough room and good relations with your neighbours, allow a strip of garden to run wild in the summer. Mow or cut it once in the spring and once in the autumn. Not only does this reduce the amount of work you have to do, it will also help bees and other insects enormously.

One aspect of management that particularly helps bees is to keep a range of flowering plants that push up blooms right through to late in the season, even into November. There are species, such as the ivy bee, that depend on the pollen on this and other flowers.

You can also invest in a bee hotel. For more information on these, see page 192.

Finally, if you get genuinely interested in bees, enough to identify some of the different species, you can join BeeWalk, the bumblebee recording scheme that assesses the abundance of these bees through the season.

Stag Beetle

Lucanus cervus

FACT FILE

DISTRIBUTION

Mainly the southern half of England and south Wales, commonest in the south-east of England. Comes out May to August.

CURRENT STATUS

Nationally scarce. Near-Threatened in Britain and Europe.

PAST AND CURRENT POPULATIONS

Unknown.

DESCRIPTION OF THE SPECIES

Large, finger-length beetle, male to 7.5cm, female to 5cm. Dark and shiny body. Males have remarkable antler-like, modified jaws.

DESCRIPTION OF THE THREATS

Overall habitat destruction, especially of ancient woodland. Tidying-up of parks and gardens, especially of stumps. Cats; road collisions; deliberate killing by terrified humans.

WHAT WE NEED TO DO

Report sightings; leave stumps and dead trees; make piles of dead branches.

ORGANISATIONS TO SUPPORT

Peoples' Trust for Endangered Species; Buglife.

CHANCES OF SURVIVAL IN BRITAIN TO 2050

4/5

This account is particularly for those in London and the Home Counties, who might feel that helping animals such as skylarks and bats is beyond them. The stag beetle's story is one that could be right up your street – literally.

This is our largest beetle and it is magnificent. Up to 7.5cm long, the males have amazing 'antlers', which look like pincers; the rest of the body is shiny dark brown and armour-plated. Females are smaller, up to 5cm long, but still hefty and although they lack the impressive antlers, they can inflict a painful nip – once again, the female of the species is more deadly …

Stag beetles lay their eggs in damp, rotting stumps of oaks and other trees, with each female laying about 70 eggs in all. These mature for up to seven years (usually 3–4), eventually making a 'cell' inside that is about the size of an orange. After hatching in the autumn, the adult makes its way out of its stump the following spring. Once abroad, it has just one job, reproduction.

This isn't easy. First, the male must find a female, presumably following a chemical trail. The trouble is, this is a big insect and, let's face it, it has spent years cooped up in the dark. Now it has to take wing on warm evenings, with a figure attuned to a wide-bodied jet, aerodynamically unpractised and easily exhausted, with a range not exceeding 1km. Once it has found a female, it might well have to fight another male for it, which is what the antlers are for. So midsummer nights can be a nightmare.

If this part goes well, the next step is also far from assured. Now the female must take flight, this time to find a place to lay eggs. Once again, given its limited powers of dispersal, finding a suitable rotting stump can be difficult.

Nobody knows how many stag beetles there used to be, but given the wholesale removal of dead stumps from all manner of places, as well as chopping down ancient woodlands, there is no doubt at all that we don't have anything like the numbers of yore. Stag beetles are endangered in much of Europe, and have actually disappeared from Latvia and Denmark. However, this is where readers in London and the south-east come in: here there are still plenty, and they need your help.

The most important thing we can all do is to be less obsessed with tidiness, both as individuals and societies. Ironically, many in the population leave litter all over the place when visiting the countryside, yet are quite happy for councils to remove old or dead trees, to tidy unsightly corners of parks and to carry out tree surgery. It happens in gardens, too. The best thing we can do, if we have a garden with old trees, is to cherish them, even as they decay – yes, make them safe, but also ensure that the beetles have a place to live.

If we wish to preserve stag beetles, we also need to join the ranks of people who advocate for them. Every year, hundreds are needlessly killed for no reason other than people finding them frightening. They are also, unfortunately, attracted to warm surfaces; when this is tarmac, it means that many are squashed by cars.

If there are stag beetles in your area, you can help them in the garden. The People's Trust for Endangered Species recommends that you leave stumps in situ to rot, and if you have a pile of logs from a lopped tree, leave them in contact with the soil and don't burn them. Also, if you can, avoid constructing decking, as this may prevent the females getting to where they need to lay eggs. During the time that beetles emerge (usually around midsummer), look out for cats and magpies on the prowl, which are predators of the beetles. Remember, these insects are useless at flying, so cover over any water butts or other water with high edges.

It is also possible to build your own stag beetle habitat, which sounds a lot of fun if you have room. Essentially, you obtain short logs from any deciduous tree and line them up, a bit like skittles.

There is one more thing you can do, which is very important. If you do have stag beetles bumbling around your garden or neighbourhood, report your sighting to the Great Stag Hunt. This will help conservationists know where the populations are, so they can concentrate their attentions to the best places. And many of these will be parks, gardens and open spaces in London.

More information can be found on the website of the People's Trust for Endangered Species (PTES).

Horrid Ground Weaver Spider

Nothophantes horridus

--- **FACT FILE** ---

DISTRIBUTION

Limestone quarries near Plymouth, Devon.

CURRENT STATUS

Critically Endangered (globally and nationally).

PAST AND CURRENT POPULATIONS

Discovered in 1995. Population unknown but must be very small (fewer than 50 have ever been seen).

DESCRIPTION OF THE SPECIES

2.5mm long money spider. Reddish brown.

DESCRIPTION OF THE THREATS

Development for housing and industrial sites.

WHAT WE NEED TO DO

Vigilance against any planning applications; lobby to make it harder for developers to resubmit planning applications; formal protection of the sites.

ORGANISATIONS TO SUPPORT

Buglife.

CHANCES OF SURVIVAL IN BRITAIN TO 2050

2/5

The only thing horrid about the horrid ground weaver spider is its survival prospects. It is only found in three sites within a single square kilometre in Plymouth, Devon – and nowhere else on our planet.

This money spider, which has a body length of only 2.5mm, was only discovered in 1995. Britain probably has the most intensively studied animal life in the world, so finding a new species for science here is a momentous event. Not only that, the spider is apparently found nowhere else but the UK, which is also very unusual; of our 670 spider species, horrid ground weaver is the only one so confined.

It is, therefore, a pretty special creature. You might think that protecting our only unique, brand-new spider would immediately be a high priority for local and regional government. However, not long after its discovery, its type locality, the place where it came to light, Shapter's Field Quarry, was built over and became the Plymouth Trade Park industrial estate. That could have been that, but fortunately the spider was rediscovered four years later at two other nearby quarries, hiding deep in cracks between the limestone blocks.

Then, in 2014, a company called Wainhomes (South West) Holdings Ltd put forward a planning application to build houses on Redford Quarry, the spider's main stronghold. For a number of months, the horrid ground weaver's survival rested in the hands of Plymouth City Council. Happily, the application was rejected. As every conservationist knows to their cost, however, developers have a strategy when it comes to rejected applications. They appealed. It is common practice for such companies to resubmit their applications again and again, until either their opponents run out of money or are exhausted by the process. On this occasion the appeal triggered a formal planning enquiry.

And then something amazing happened. The charity Buglife, alarmed by the spider's fate, began an online petition in 2015 to gather support to save the horrid ground weaver from extinction; it garnered 10,000 signatures. Buglife then began a crowdsourcing campaign to raise money to fund ecological studies on the spider and promote its conservation. Remarkably it raised over £10,000. At about the same time the global body International Union for Conservation of Nature (IUCN) placed the horrid ground weaver on its list of threatened species as Critically Endangered. For once, with all the publicity in its favour, the money was on the money spider.

In June 2015 the planning inspector rejected the builder's application on the grounds that it would harm diversity. The decision was particularly unusual and welcome because the quarry had no formal protection, not even as a Site of Special Scientific Importance. Nevertheless, the quarry is safe for now. In 2016, the spider was found for the first time at a fourth location – with delightful irony, at an industrial site.

Nevertheless, the situation for the horrid ground weaver spider is still parlous. Almost nothing is known about it, so we don't yet know what its ecological requirements are. Without this information, and without knowing how many spiders are out there, we simply cannot foretell what new threats might come in the future. It is in the balance.

But the story of the horrid ground weaver spider should also be encouraging. Spiders as a group aren't popular, on the whole, and virtually nobody has ever seen this retiring nocturnal invertebrate. It isn't horrid (the name comes from the Latin *horridus*, meaning 'bristly') but it is hardly conventionally beautiful. Yet 10,000 people cared enough to sign a petition in its favour, and people put their hands in their pockets to help save it. Its rarity and eye-catching name undoubtedly helped, but it does show that popular support on social media can have a powerful effect.

Pink Sea Fan

Eunicella verrucosa

FACT FILE

DISTRIBUTION

In water over 10m depth in south-west England, Wales, southern Ireland and Channel Islands.

CURRENT STATUS

Nationally Scarce, Vulnerable.

PAST AND CURRENT POPULATIONS

Unknown, but there may be half a million colonies in Lyme Bay, Dorset/Devon.

DESCRIPTION OF THE SPECIES

The colonies on rocks live up to their name, fan-like structures with branches. Maximum 30cm tall and 40cm wide. Not always pink, sometimes white or yellow.

DESCRIPTION OF THE THREATS

Breakage by divers; disease; but especially trawling and scallop dredging.

WHAT WE NEED TO DO

Regulate scallop dredging and ban the most destructive practices.

ORGANISATIONS TO SUPPORT

Marine Conservation Society; MARINElife.

CHANCES OF SURVIVAL IN BRITAIN TO 2050

5/5

I t sounds like something out of a children's book, but the pink sea fan is a real animal of our marine environment. It is related to a raft of cool animals such as corals, sea anemones, jellyfish and hydras, all of which come under the umbrella term of cnidarians, united by bearing special prey-catching cells called cnidocytes. Sea fans are colonies of polyps that branch out like fans, supported by a branched skeleton of hard protein. They grow at right angles to the sea current, so that as the water passes, they can catch prey items such as plankton in their tiny tentacles.

Sea fans are slow-growing, only adding about a centimetre a year to their overall size, and many large colonies are decades old. They live in shallow waters, typically growing off flat bedrock or the flatter parts of wrecks in areas with a strong current. In some areas, 'forests' of sea fans grow in close proximity, sometimes as many as 20 per square metre, one of the great sights of the British marine environment. To most people, they are the stuff not of experience, but of wildlife documentaries.

The pink sea fan is a charismatic member of our undersea heritage, which overall is incredibly rich. It so happens that two other animals are strongly associated with these sea fans, one of two species in Britain (the other is the northern sea fan, which is friendlier and has a different accent); these are a sea slug with the slightly fruity name of whip fan nudibranch *Tritonia nilsodhneri*, and the sea fan anemone *Amphianthus dohmii*. The sea slug is camouflaged to look like a sea fan, a great example of the intricate ecology of the seabed. Cat-sharks also attach their eggs in their mermaid's purses to sea fan branches.

The pink sea fan is one of the few marine animals protected under the Wildlife and Countryside Act, so it is illegal to damage or disturb them. It is also part of the UK's Biodiversity Action Plan. That is a lot of attention for a cnidarian that is still relatively common. However, the sea fan is a good example of an animal that, should it be afflicted with some kind of local disaster, is unlikely to recover quickly, if at all. In the past, divers would often bring up sea fans as souvenirs. When this happened, it would take years for the colony to re-establish itself. The reproductive larvae of sea fans disperse on the currents but are probably non-feeding and don't live for very long, which is also a problem, meaning that sea fans are not very good at dispersing. They may take four years to reach a wreck 50m away, and if a suitable seabed is more than a kilometre away, they may never reach it at all.

Their slow growth and poor dispersal make sea fans highly vulnerable. Although we do not know as much about what human activities do to the marine environment as the land environment, the sea fan is one of those animals that could very easily disappear if we aren't careful.

And the trouble is, we do interfere with the seabed. The occasional diver might accidently break a colony, and oil and other pollution could potentially cause wipe-outs. But the biggest threat to sea fans is bottom-trawling for fish and, particularly, scallop-dredging.

Dredging for scallops is a boon commercially for many fishermen in the winter, but it can also be extraordinarily destructive. Scallops live on the seabed immersed in sand, and the only way to reach them is to pull a horizontal metal beam fitted with teeth behind a boat to scour the seabed, its net trailing behind. The method smashes the seabed; hundreds of creatures are gouged out as bycatch, along with the precious shellfish. It is highly destructive, the grouse-shooting of the sea, when the environment is sacrificed for a single cause with economic power.

In a perfect world, scallop dredging would not be allowed anywhere. In reality, it needs to be accommodated. There are many stories of scallop boats dredging illegally in protected areas, and this should be penalised with stiff fines. Otherwise, the only protection from the destruction is to have properly protected Marine Protection Zones. Those Zones with pink sea fans should not be exploited for scallops or bottom-dwelling fish. There should also be a network of well-policed No Take Zones. The Marine Conservation Society are monitoring some populations carefully, and also carrying out research to show the effects of the destruction by bottom-trawling and dredging.

There is another thing that anybody can do, and that is to care where your scallops come from. It so happens that scallops can be caught by divers by hand, with minimal destruction of the seabed. If consumers began to insist that their shellfish and bottom-dwelling fish were caught in sustainable ways, rapacious hunters would be pressured into changing their ways.

Earthworm
(Common Lobworm)

Lumbricus terrestris

FACT FILE

DISTRIBUTION

Soil throughout the UK. There are 29 species of earthworms in Britain.

CURRENT STATUS

Abundant.

PAST AND CURRENT POPULATIONS

Unknown.

DESCRIPTION OF THE SPECIES

Lobworm is a large worm up to 35cm long, with a generously plump, cylindrical body with a pink/purple tinge. Tail is the shape of a flattened paddle. Sexually mature individuals have saddle in the middle.

DESCRIPTION OF THE THREATS

May be affected by pesticides and herbicides in soil; soil compaction; erosion; miscellaneous contamination.

WHAT WE NEED TO DO

Fill in gaps in knowledge. Above all, monitor what might be going on in our soils.

ORGANISATIONS TO SUPPORT

Earthworm Society of Britain.

CHANCES OF SURVIVAL IN BRITAIN TO 2050

5/5 (or we're all dead)

Earthworms are like domestic chores: they are not very exciting, but they are very important. Worms don't have much character, and not a shred of glamour, yet we couldn't survive without them. They eat dead and decaying plants, such as leaves, releasing nutrients into the soil as their excreta and keeping it fertile. By tunnelling through the earth, they allow oxygen into the soil and passageways for water to leak through, effectively acting as ploughing agents underground. They help to mix soil layers, and without them it would be lifeless and compacted. Without rich soils we couldn't grow crops. To humans, worms are among the most important animals in the world. It has been estimated (who knows how?) that worms contribute £16 billion a year to UK agriculture.

But how much attention do worms receive? When did you last see a worm? It was presumably when you were digging the garden. Are you a worm-friendly person? Have you ever checked your worm population?

No? Well, don't worry; not many people ever have counted worms in the way that they count birds or butterflies. Only very recently has anyone even thought about the conservation of worms. You don't get many appeals in the post about helping worms.

For a start, what animals are we talking about? A worm isn't just a worm; there are ten or so species that occur commonly in gardens. The common lobworm is the most frequently seen species, although it is often witnessed being pulled from its burrow by a blackbird or being cut in half by your spade. This species is one that, as if by magic, pulls those fallen autumn leaves down into the ground. In wet weather at night it hauls itself to the surface to look for a mate, then entwines itself with another individual, hermaphrodite to hermaphrodite. A good garden soil is now known to hold around 20–40 worms per square metre.

There are other species. The deep-burrowing long worm (*Aporrectodea longa*), which looks like a lobworm on a diet, is the one that annoyingly leaves worm-casts on lawns. The brandling (*Eisenia fetida*) produces a foul-smelling yellow fluid when it is handled. There are grey worms, green worms, red worms and tiger worms. The various species can be divided into four working groups: *epigeic* worms live at the surface and break down leaf-litter; *endogeic* worms live in soil, eating it and ploughing through it; *anecic* worms pull the leaves down into the soil to eat; and *composting* worms specialise in rotting vegetation. They all do an incredible job, though. Really, we should go on to the streets and clap them every week.

It is, of course, in our interest that worms are flourishing, but we are only just beginning to find out more about their abundance. For example, they simply adore organic compost, so a compost heap in a garden makes them leap with joy, or would if they could. Surface-feeding earthworms are especially abundant under hedges and shrubs, in view of the large amount of litter below them. And they prefer clay soils to sandy soils. There is some evidence that worms are found in lower density in arable farmland soils. This wouldn't be surprising, in view of how poor arable land is for other wildlife; having to cope with 20 sprays of pesticides or herbicides a year must be a challenge. But the truth is that we don't really know if this is a serious problem or not.

One thing we do know is that earthworms love gardens above every other habitat in Britain, perhaps because of the variety of land uses in a small area, and the likelihood of compost heaps. Plant pots, a garden staple, are good hideaways, and piles of logs that are allowed to decay into the soil will significantly increase a garden's overall worm richness.

There is much more you can do – and avoid – to help your earthworms. Try mulching your leaves and spreading them over the soil and add natural compost from your heap whenever you are turning over the soil. As always – a suggestion you will see continually throughout this book – avoid adding chemicals such as slug pellets. Another – don't, whatever you do, put a plastic covering such as AstroTurf over your lawn, and where possible avoid paving.

Worms are, of course, the ultimate soil animals, so it is worth mentioning here that there is something of a soil crisis in Britain at the moment, especially in agricultural areas which is, ahem, 70% of the whole country. Government estimates suggest that intensive agriculture has caused arable soils to lose about 40–60% of their organic carbon, while 4 million hectares of soil are at risk of compaction and 2 million of erosion. 300,000 hectares are contaminated and nobody even knows what effect large amounts of microplastics in the soil might have. In 2017, Michael Gove, launching the Sustainable Soils Alliance, declared that the UK is only 30–40 years away from 'the fundamental eradication of soil fertility' in some places. In 2014 researchers from Sheffield University concluded that UK soils only have 100 harvests left in them.

These are sobering thoughts. Intensive agriculture, which started with such good intentions, has become a desperate problem.

Fortunately, however, our gardens are likely always to be refuges for all kinds of soil invertebrates, not just worms. So, follow the advice above and the general garden advice (see especially page 184).

And while you're about it, why not join the Earthworm Society of Britain? Apart from doing some fantastic work to publicise worms and make people love them, saying you're a member is a great opening line at a party.

Cornflower

Centaurea cyanus

DISTRIBUTION

Might hold on somewhere wild in an English cornfield. Widely planted, so quite common. Flowers from June to August.

CURRENT STATUS

Probably extinct as original archaeophyte (see text that follows). Common otherwise.

PAST AND CURRENT POPULATIONS

Unknown.

DESCRIPTION OF THE SPECIES

Tall upright flower growing to 80cm. Vibrant blue flowerhead with enlarged outer florets, 15–30mm across.

DESCRIPTION OF THE THREATS

Extreme intensive arable farming, including herbicide use and cleaning of corn seeds.

WHAT WE NEED TO DO

Too late for original population in Britain, but easily reintroduced from seed mixes, including to wildflower strips.

ORGANISATIONS TO SUPPORT

Plantlife.

CHANCES OF SURVIVAL IN BRITAIN TO 2050

0.5/5 (5/5 in seed mixes)

Britain's flowers deserve a big hurrah. We have about 2500 native flowering plants, which includes trees and shrubs, in this country. They range from the beautiful to the even more so. Imagine life without them. Country verges would be bare or soulless. There would be no bluebell woods and no summer meadows, our kitchens would be without herbs and spices. Imagine life without buttercups, daisies, mint, gorse, speedwells, orchids, scarlet pimpernel and corky-fruited water-dropwort (well, maybe not that one). Imagine the tedious late winter months without snowdrops, celandines and daffodils. Imagine midsummer arable fields without the bleeding blooms of poppies. As it happens, all grasses are flowering plants too, and without these (rice, wheat, barley) the human race would struggle to survive.

Needless to say, in Britain, in our rush for economic progress and high-end lifestyle, we have neglected our flora as much as our fauna, especially since the Second World War. We have ploughed wildflower meadows; we have concreted over flower-rich habitats; we have poisoned flowers with herbicide; we have tidied up wildflowers from corners. It is estimated that, every single year, a flower species is lost from a county in Britain. It is a scandal, but you will rarely, if ever, hear a chorus of politicians voicing grave concern. You might say we have kicked the problem into the, er, long grass. The trouble is, even the long grass at the edge of a field is now a colourless apology of what it could and should be.

The cornflower is a symbol of a lost Britain. It is what is known in botanical circles as an archaeophyte, a plant with a particularly fascinating past. It is unlikely to be native to Britain but was introduced here by ancient farmers and has definitively been on our islands since the Iron Age (500 BC to AD 800). Admittedly, it is a weed, a hanger-on to cultivation. But it has flowers of the kind of blue that make you wish to sing out loud. You can see from the images shown here.

In days gone by, cornflowers adorned the edges of arable crops and sometimes were interlopers throughout. Imagine that – an entire field of cornflowers stretching out to the horizon, just as there are poppy fields that turn parts of England crimson in June. Think of that ethereal blue. Throughout Europe, this botanical nuisance became one of the most popular of all flowers. It is the national flower of Estonia and a huge favourite in Germany and France. There is a long tradition that smitten young men would wear cornflowers to test the desire of their fancies; a faded cornflower would be a warning of unrequited love. Van Gogh painted *Wheat Field with Cornflowers* in July 1890 in celebration of a field at Auvers-sur-Oise in France. How the colour must have lifted the spirits on summer days. Up until the war years, it was still possible to see fields like this in Britain.

Cornflowers, the weeds, were always the by-product of inefficiency, the symbol of imperfection. But after the Second World War, arable farming in Britain embraced efficiency, becoming intensive and increasingly intolerant. It was perhaps a necessity, at least at first, and improved productivity is hardly an ill per se. But it could be argued that, while the necessity waned, intensification intensified and has never stopped. Meadows went under the plough. Field edges were ruthlessly straightened out for incremental increases in yield. Crop intruders were poisoned by herbicides, while the crops themselves were bred to be fast-growing and muscular, fertilised to within an inch of their lives. Seed-corn cleaning sifted the seeds of unwanted weeds out. The result is a deeply unnatural set of monocultures, with a crash in biodiversity. Our countryside is green, pleasant and, other than crops, barely alive.

The cornflower and its archaeophyte ilk buckled under this series of agricultural aggravations, crushed like dissidents in a police state. In a world of intensive agriculture, there is little room for anything else except the product. Within a few short years, cornflowers withered away. By the end of the 1970s, the species had become nationally scarce. True wild populations of cornflowers are today in danger of extinction, except for the occasional appearance of flowers from deeply buried seeds. We will never see the fields again.

You might be frowning at this point and saying to yourself: 'I'm sure I've seen this flower around.' And you'd be right. These days, the seeds of cornflower are an integral part of flower meadow seed mixes, which are available everywhere. Many councils plant these mixes on verges and other public amenity areas, so it is likely that you have seen patches of cornflowers about your area. Various varieties are also popular in gardens. However, this is very much a career change for this flower, and it is unsustainable outside deliberate plantings. In botanical terms, the cornflower has switched from an archaeophyte to a neophyte, a new alien arrival.

And while we are likely to keep seeing cornflowers on our verges and roundabouts, the basic problem of our arable monocultures remains. There is nothing anybody can do to bring back the cornflower, and several other species, to their former glory. However, restoring some of the arable bystanders is possible.

A new project has been launched by Plantlife's Back from the Brink Initiative to survey arable farmland, restore strips of wildflowers and reconnect people with the farmed environment. Cleverly entitled Colour in the Margins, it is asking for help from volunteers mainly, at this early stage, to monitor a selection of sites to find out what is already there.

If you are interested in wildflowers, follow #wildflowerhour on Twitter.

Yellow Rattle

Rhinanthus minor

FACT FILE

DISTRIBUTION

Throughout British Isles in lowland and upland grassland. Flowers from May to September.

CURRENT STATUS

Least Concern.

PAST AND CURRENT POPULATIONS

Unknown, but decreased.

DESCRIPTION OF THE SPECIES

Grows to 50cm, upright and often in patches. Resembles unrelated dead-nettle but with yellow jaw-like flowers 12–15mm across. Sepals expand to inflated sacs after flowers, seeds rattle within. Serrated leaves.

DESCRIPTION OF THE THREATS

Destruction of hay meadows and other habitats.

WHAT WE NEED TO DO:

Re-sow meadows, including in gardens.

ORGANISATIONS TO SUPPORT

Plantlife.

CHANCES OF SURVIVAL IN BRITAIN TO 2050

5/5

I t might be a scene from a bygone age. A family walks through a meadow in August, enjoying the fresh air and sun. Amidst the sun-blasted stems of grass below their feet are military straight stands of dead-looking plants laden with swollen, tired-brown blisters. 'What's this flower?' ask the children.

'Pick one and shake it to find out,' replies a parent. The youngster does so and a smile forms across her face as the pleasing rattling noise emanates from the seed case. 'It's called hay-rattle,' replies the parent. 'Once this flower's seeds are rattling like this, the farmer knows that it's time to harvest.'

The hay-rattle, better known as yellow rattle, is a flower of the meadows. In pre-war years it must have been one of the commonest plants in Britain, and conversations similar to the above would have taken place frequently among a rural community that knew their flowers intimately. However, like the elms whose wispy foliage decorate the paintings of John Constable and his contemporaries, the yellow rattle no longer frames the countryside. The old meadows that were once a vital part of the rural economy have largely vanished. They have been replaced by grasslands that are dubiously called 'improved'. They are not an improvement in most senses of the word. They are just another by-product of more intensive agriculture.

In 1930, Britain had about 7 million hectares of semi-natural grassland, which was cut as hay in the late summer to feed animals. Today, an incredible 97% has been lost, and much of what remains is in tiny patches. After the wars, farmers were encouraged to add fertiliser and to plough (a subsidy was granted to encourage this), with the result that only 30% remained by 1971. Now there are 10,500 hectares of lowland meadow and 900 hectares of upland hay meadows. The problem is that grassland that has been 'improved' for agricultural yields has impoverished biodiversity. Semi-natural hay meadows have many times the number of plant species growing on them. They don't just look more beautiful.

For years, conservationists were slow to prioritise grassland, except for chalk grasslands, which had also been widely ploughed in the post-war years. It is only since the 1980s that they have received the attention they deserve. And remarkably, owing to the efforts of conservationists and changing attitudes towards meadows, they are making a comeback. And part of this is the fashion towards wildflower meadows in gardens.

Wildflower meadows are quite difficult to establish. The grass on your lawn probably consists of species such as rye-grass which thrive in the rich soil, grow quickly, and can easily overpower the flowers you want to grow and turn it into a biodiversity cold-spot. You could remove the excessive nutrients in your lawn by scraping off the overlying topsoil to reveal the poorer soil beneath, but this is a laborious, difficult process. To get the best meadows you must halt any mowing between May and at least August, by which time your sward will be tall and difficult to cut. It is worth persisting, though, as there is a ready-made helper for everybody who wants a meadow – yellow rattle.

Yellow rattle is not a normal flower. Not for the yellow rattle that tiresome business of growing big leaves and getting its energy by photosynthesis from the sun. No, this attractive flower is what is known as a hemi-parasite. Although it can grow by itself, more often than not it flourishes on the efforts of other plants, by bleeding their water and minerals. It inveigles its root system into theirs and sucks them dry. And guess which plants it attacks in this way – grasses, of which rye-grass is one.

The yellow rattle, therefore, that plant that has diminished as the meadows have disappeared, is literally leading their recovery. Wildflower mixes almost invariably have yellow rattle within them, and these greatly diminish the time it takes to get your meadow flowery and colourful. You take the mix, shake out the rattle and roll with it.

What We Can Do

CONVENTIONAL GARDENING

Not everyone has a garden. If you don't, or don't have access to any land over which you have jurisdiction, have a look at the section in this book, 'Unconventional Gardening' (page 204).

If you have read any sections of this book and they have made your blood boil, and you are angry at the overall reduction and abuse of wildlife, there is somewhere you can turn to – your own garden. There are around 200 million homes in Britain (including second homes), and 90% of these have some form of garden. Although that number is steadily diminishing, that is still a great deal of land. If it was all managed for wildlife, it would be incredible. And whatever might be happening in your neighbourhood, at least you, as a conservationist, can do your bit and salve your conscience. The wildlife will benefit.

This section assumes that you would like to manage your garden for maximum advantage for wildlife. In practice, of course, you can't do everything. A certain consideration for your neighbours, and a nod to tidiness, might actually convince those around you that wildlife gardening is not as risky and scandalous as they might have expected.

Before we begin, I need to recommend a book that will change your attitude to gardens and wildlife. *The Garden Jungle: or Gardening to Save the Planet* by Dave Goulson will give much excellent advice in much more detail than here.

Here, then, are some practical suggestions for making your garden better for wildlife.

KEEP YOUR LAWN

Lawns are very good for wildlife, but they are becoming less and less popular. Presumably, the idea of mowing occasionally or even, perish the thought, accepting occasionally that the children or dog will bring in grass or mud, is anathema to the modern household. Besides, why spend time cutting the grass in the fresh air when you could be checking your emails? The result is a terrible concreting over, or decking over, or, worst of all, putting in artificial grass. A survey ten years ago found that two-thirds of London's front gardens are at least partially covered by surfacing other than vegetation. This is a disaster. If you want a plastic lawn, you might as well have plastic flowers.

ACCEPT THE POSSIBILITY OF UNTIDINESS

There is no doubt that a manicured garden, in which every corner is beautiful, looks great, and it might be perfectly reasonable for wildlife. However, if you care about conservation, you want something a little better than reasonable: you want a great wildlife garden. Unfortunately, garden wildlife likes mess. Hedgehogs like long grass, almost everything likes brambles and nettles, and insects revel in decay, dirtiness and neglected corners. The ideal garden needs at least some imperfection.

PLANT LOTS OF FLOWERS

They look wonderful, and the sheer feast for the eyes boosts our mental health. And the great thing is, they are also fantastic for insects such as bees, hoverflies, butterflies and moths. Select lots of different ones and, if you can, make sure to plant as many flowers for pollinators as possible. Dave Goulson suggests that you go to a garden centre on a fine day and spend a few moments seeing which flowers are most frequently visited, and buy those. Another good tip is to get cuttings and pot plants from your neighbours.

CHANGE YOUR ATTITUDE TO WEEDS

To many gardeners, although now a dwindling number, weeds are plants in the wrong place. You plant a flowerbed for your dahlias and, low and behold, groundsel and dandelions grow up alongside them, uninvited. If you take the most extreme view, though, what's the difference? Well, dahlias are attractive, definitely more so than groundsel. But groundsel and dandelions are both edible; dandelion tea is delicious, and you can add the leaves of both of these weeds to salad. Dandelions are also superb for insect pollinators such as bees. I am not saying that you should abandon any kind of planting, and plants such as thistles and brambles can quickly take over if neglected, but I am suggesting that humble 'weeds' should be allowed into gardens. If you allow a weed patch, you can always rename it your wildflower garden.

ADD A WATER FEATURE

Preferably add a pond. In the countryside at large, ponds are disappearing. You can make good this lack by constructing your own. The wildlife gains are simply incredible.

STAY FREE OF CHEMICALS

Be organic in your garden if you possibly can. Pesticides and herbicides are – and the suffix '-cide' is the clue because it means 'kill' – poisons. They are built to destroy. Their long-term effects are rarely fully studied, and those used in farming turn up in many unexpected places, not least our food and our water. Slug pellets kill slugs and what eats slugs? Hedgehogs. Fill in the blanks. Yes, it's annoying when aphids eat your broad beans, but in the long term, if you encourage ladybirds by not poisoning your garden, the ladybirds will probably do the job for you.

MAKE A COMPOST HEAP

There is more information about these on the section on slow worms (see page 99). Compost heaps are easy to construct and look after and have endless benefits to wildlife.

If you don't have your own compost heap, make sure that you use peat-free compost. This is absolutely essential, because the cutting of peat in Scotland to provide to garden centres is a national scandal. Peat is a habitat that builds up for thousands of years and provides superb and unique habitat for much wildlife. It also traps a great deal of carbon. Make sure that your compost comes from a source, such as the RHS, that doesn't exploit this habitat.

SOURCE YOUR FLOWERS CAREFULLY

Garden centres sell a lot of flowers, but many are imported from Europe and treated with chemicals. If you can, why not try to source your plants either from a specialist nursery that is free of chemicals, or even from your friends and neighbours? They are often only too glad to share their blooms with you and you can return the favour. And it's much cheaper. What's not to like?

PROVIDING HOMES FOR WILDLIFE

A good wildlife-friendly garden organically provides resources for many animals, from bees to hedgehogs. However, one particular delight in wildlife gardening comes from putting up, or even creating, suitable feeders and lodgings for them. There is nothing quite like putting work into creating a bird table or nest box and then seeing customers come and go. Many pieces of such wildlife kit are widely available commercially, too, of course, and you can still get much pleasure from watching them being used.

BIRD BOX

Nest boxes are genuinely helpful to birds. Several of our common species, notably tits, otherwise depend on wild holes in trees and elsewhere for nesting sites, which are always at a premium, so providing artificial boxes helps to satisfy the great demand.

Siting is very important in two respects – make sure it isn't facing south into the sun, or you might inadvertently overheat the eggs or young on a hot day; and secondly, make sure it is out of reach of cats and other predators. Otherwise, trying to second-guess why birds choose particular sites is futile. They often occupy places we might deem unsuitable! They certainly don't care a jot about a neat and beautiful design, even if you do. The rule is, don't expect perfection; it isn't there in nature.

- Use wood such as pine which doesn't warp. You don't need much; try to use offcuts.
- Timber should be at least 15mm thick so that it's warm enough inside for the chicks.

- Paint the exterior of the box with water-based preservative, otherwise it will quickly rot. Don't paint the inside.
- Add extra weatherproofing to the roof. The roof should overhang the entrance if possible. Put a hinge in so that you can open the roof for monitoring and cleaning.
- Make sure you drill holes in the base to allow drainage.
- Clean after 1 September.

Don't make the box too big. A plank size of about 150mm × 1170mm will be sufficient.

Try a tit box first, as this is the most likely to be successful. For blue tits, a round hole of 25mm diameter in the front near the top is just right.

Other hole sizes: great tit 28mm, house sparrow 32mm.

For robins, you will need an open-fronted design. Instead of a closed front with a hole cut, the top half of the front is left open.

OWL BOX

The same rules apply to owls that apply to tits; supply is inevitably lower than demand. So, putting up a box for an owl can benefit the birds in the wild considerably, and this applies particularly to the barn owl. The advice here applies to that species. Any information you require in addition can be found on the Barn Owl Trust website.

- Siting is very important for barn owls, and the very best sites are indoors, in buildings with easy access such as, well, barns. According to the Barn Owl Trust, modern barns are perfect for nest boxes, but without one provided most owls ignore them.
- There cannot be enough boxes made for these birds.

- You can also site the box in a tree, or even on a purpose-built pole.
- Use FSC-approved plywood of minimum 9mm diameter. You'll also need batten of 50 × 25mm.

A barn owl box is obviously much bigger than a tit box! 50cm wide × 40cm × 60cm is a minimum requirement.

The entrance hole is usually square (13cm × 13cm minimum) and set close to the roof.

The biggest difference is that the box needs an exercise ledge for the owlets to use just below the entrance.

Designs and tips are available on the Barn Owl Trust website.

DORMOUSE BOXES

Even if you have never seen a dormouse in your life, and don't live near a colony, you can still make a difference to this animal's conservation by making your own boxes or buying them for your local dormouse group. Imagine how it would feel if this glorious, fast-declining rodent was to bring up a brood inside a box made by your own hand? That would be wonderful.

The big difference between a dormouse box and a bird box is that the dormouse box has a hole in the back, not the front. The rodent enters directly from the tree trunk and doesn't peer out the front.

Dormouse boxes tend not to be used straight away and may only be occupied after a few seasons. For this reason, they need to be made of wood that is resistant to rotting. They must not be treated with any preservative or weatherproofing.

- 28mm diameter for hole.
- Top must be easily removable for monitoring.

- Larch or red cedar is best medium.
- Wood should be 12–16cm thick.
- Top should be held shut with wire attached to screw at the back.

For detailed instructions, see the People's Trust for Endangered Species (PTES) website.

SWIFT BOX

Swifts are another species for which a lack of breeding spaces is crucial. You can make a simple box yourself. Be aware that it might take a long time to be used, and if you play recordings of screaming swifts from it, the birds are more likely to come to check it out.

Precise instructions are on the RSPB website.

- Make sure you can site it high enough off ground, at least 5m up on the side of a building, with an unobstructed flight path. Under the eaves is often ideal.
- Use a responsibly sourced sheet of plywood of 1800mm long × 150mm wide × 12–18mm thick.
- Hole needs to be 77mm wide and 40mm high.
- Use screws to attach the front so that the nest can be cleaned out (October).

BAT BOX

Bat boxes should be everywhere, because these wonderful mammals use them all the time for both breeding and, sometimes, hibernating. The delightful thing about bat boxes, unlike other boxes for wildlife, is that a whole colony might settle into something you have made yourself!

Remember that it is illegal to disturb bats at the roost unless you have a licence. This applies even if you have built the box yourself, without anybody else knowing. Bats usually emerge at regular times each evening, so you might still be able to see if it is occupied.

Bat boxes are those odd boxes that have no entrance hole in the middle. Instead, the bats come in and out using a slit at the bottom.

- You'll need untreated wood.
- Rough-sawn wood is needed.
- In contrast to many other nest boxes, a large one is better than a small one.
- Make sure it is draught-proof.
- It must be sited at least 3m above the ground.
- Place it on a tree in your garden, or local wood, or wherever you have permission to put it up.
- It can also be sited on the wall of a building.
- It must have a removable top for monitoring (but see above).

HEDGEHOG HOME

You can build a home for hedgehogs. In fact, there are two types, luxury and bargain. As far as the spiny mammals are concerned, they aren't fussed. And they do seem to work. A customer survey found that, of those who responded about the boxes, 59% found the hogs using them for hibernation and 28% for breeding. So, in these hard times for hedgehogs, it seems a good thing to provide.

Hedgehog boxes need an access tunnel to keep out dogs and badgers, leading to a large interior. Placed on the ground, they need to be reasonably robust.

- Place on the ground under the shade of a shrub, in a quiet part of the garden away from the house.
- The main interior should be about 30cm × 40cm

Hedgehog Luxury House
- Made of untreated plywood of 20mm thickness.
- Birch is recommended as a source; try to obtain locally.
- The tunnel should be 30cm long, with the top and base 17cm wide and the sides 13cm high, to make the tunnel enclosed.
- Front needs to accommodate tunnel entrance, so cut out a 17cm square from one side.
- Top will require two hinges to open it for cleaning purposes.
- Place newspapers, dry leaves and grass inside.
- Cover the top with polythene, and maybe some soil.
- Add indoor cinema, coffee machine and widescreen TV, according to your hedgehogs' tastes.

Hedgehog 'Bargain Dwelling'
This is a modified plastic storage container. It is a simplified home without a tunnel, so only use in areas without badgers.
- Take a medium-sized container and cut a hole 15cm × 15cm in the middle.
- Cut a 15cm × 5cm groove in one side for ventilation.
- Add the leaves and grass.
- Put an opened carrier bag over the top.
- Site under a shrub and cover with more grass, leaves or twigs.

HEDGEHOG TUNNEL

The average hedgehog roams 2km a night, so in the patchwork of gardens where hedgehogs still thrive, fences and other barriers can prove to be something of a headache for them. They do climb quite well, but one way of making your local hogs' life easier is to provide access between gardens.

Typically, all you have to do if you have wooden fences – and make sure that your neighbours know about it and approve – is to cut a small section off at ground level. 13cm × 13cm in sufficient and shouldn't be too obvious. Use sandpaper to make the cut look neat.

Some neighbourhoods have formed interconnected garden networks this way. See the website of the Hedgehog Street conservation initiative for details.

BEE HOTELS

The best possible thing you can do for the bees in your garden is to plant a rich range of flowers that send out blooms for the spring, summer and autumn. That will keep them more than happy.

However, you can also provide what are known as bee hotels. The rich possibilities for puns are everywhere – 'Bee B&Bs', 'Buzz Stops' and so on – if there's no other reason to have them. They don't always work, but when they do, they are truly enjoyable to watch.

The bees you are hoping to house are not the honeybees that everybody knows. Those live in big hives with thousands of workers, and they have an unpleasant sting that can cause a serious reaction in some people. They are not to be messed with and require training to look after. No, the bees that we are hoping to help are solitary bees, of which quite a few species occur in gardens and open spaces.

A bee hotel is similar to a bird nest-box placed on the side of a building or a tree – remember, these animals don't normally sting people and so having them near the house isn't a problem. However, a bee box is entirely open fronted. It is stuffed with hollow tubes, such as the cut ends of cane, dead plant stems and drilled twigs piled on top of each other. Each tube, one end flush to the back of the box and the other facing outwards, can be home to a solitary bee; that's all they need. They aren't too bothered about having neighbours, so each box can indeed be a hotel, with many residents, even of different species.

- When making your box, divide it into several compartments (three is sufficient) so that you don't have to stuff all the tubes into one large space, and can experiment with different tube diameters and lodgings.
- Although you can acquire tubes for your hotel, such as bamboo canes, it is quite fun to get them from the environment. Reed stems are a possibility. Each tube should be 3–10mm in diameter.
- The timber for the main box needs to be 15mm thick. Please use sustainably sourced wood with FSC logo.
- The box should be about 15cm deep, and thus the tubes must be cut to this length.
- Boxes can be vertical or horizontal, it doesn't matter.
- Tidiness isn't necessary.
- Don't expect instant results. You know you've been successful when the bees are flying in and out.

BUG MANSIONS

These are bee hotels gone mad. Once you understand the concept of providing tubes and homes for insects, the sky is the limit. Bug mansions are usually made very simply by laying a few pallets on top of each other on the ground, separated by bricks, and then the gaps are filled with the hollow tubes and bamboo canes, sticks, leaves, plastic bottles, cardboard, stones, bark, tiles – just about anything. They don't need much DIY skill to make.

Bug mansions are something to put at the bottom of the garden. They are undoubtedly great for invertebrates, but if you are sensitive about your garden looking gorgeous, you might want to place it out of sight.

One modified bug mansion, particularly beloved by stag beetles, is a pile of adjacent vertically positioned dead logs and stems, which may lean together to form a wigwam shape. Dead logs are a fabulous habitat in their own right.

MAKING A FLOWER MEADOW

If you have enough room in your garden, a wildflower meadow is perfect gift to the wildlife around you. A mature meadow will resound to the sound of buzzing and chirping insects in the summer, will be shimmering with brilliantly colourful butterfly wings and will be a riot of colour. And you can sit back by it or in it and admire your handiwork.

Not everybody can do this; you need a decent-sized plot. You can also plant meadow flowers in your flowerbeds. But there is something different about a meadow, even a small one.

Attitudes to wildflower meadows in gardens are changing. There was a time not so long ago when allowing 'weeds' to grow on your lawn was frowned upon, and the idea of not mowing the grass was positively scandalous. Those days are passing, and the sheer good sense of laying a flower meadow is beginning to gain traction. Meadows are beautiful, and if they are well looked after they can be sculpted easily into the rest of the garden. For example, if you make a large meadow, why not mow a walkway going tastefully and sinuously through it? Or put gravel around the edge. This way your meadow will look like an intentional and looked after part of the garden.

You shouldn't assume, though, that creating a meadow is easy. If you think you can just leave the lawn and let the grasses grow naturally, that is unlikely to work. You'll get a lot of tall grass and very little colour. The secret of laying a meadow is, counterintuitively, to make your lawn less fertile. Rank grasses are adapted to thrive in such topsoils and will invariably take over if left alone. You need to make the habitat less suitable for them.

If you are making a small patch, you can do this by simply pulling out any weeds from your chosen area and the covering the ground for about three months (from January to March, say) with black plastic. It looks horrible but is necessary. More laboriously, you can take the topsoil away, removing the top 6–10cm, and again, leave for about six weeks. If anything grows up, you can remove it. Once this time period has elapsed, hoe the bare soil to prepare it for seeding.

Then scatter a mix of seeds and rake or roll them in. There are many different wildflower meadow mixes; try to use one containing native flowers. There is a great resource for choosing native plants on the Plantlife website. Make sure you include the seeds of yellow rattle (see page 178) as this will keep the grasses down if the latter have the temerity to infiltrate your project. The best mixes for newly tilled soil are those of 'cornfield annuals', which will probably include cornflower (see page 172).

This is the point at which you hope for a good mixture of rain and sunshine. Should this happen, in a few weeks your meadow will turn colourful. Cornfield annuals are adapted to sow easily and grow quickly, so although it won't look like the end product, it will resemble what it is, a start.

The most enjoyable bit comes next. Although you might want to re-sow the proto-meadow a few times during the summer, what you will not need to do is mow it. To misquote the *Frozen* movie, 'Let it grow.' After all, 'You are one with the wind and sky.' Remember all those weeks during innumerable summers when the grass seemed to grow while you were watching it, and mowing the lawn was like an itch you needed to scratch constantly? Not any more. The sound of mowers starting up on a sunny Sunday morning, together with gardeners' grunts, is now something you can enjoy.

The one time one man (or woman) and their dog goes to mow a meadow is late August, at the end of the season. The beauty of this is that most of your plants will have set seed of their own accord and dropped them into the soil. Once you have mown it, make sure that you rake away the trimmings. If you leave them, they will rot into the soil and add to its fertility, giving your unwanted grasses, thistles and other hoi polloi a leg up for next year. Once you have mown, you might want to sow again, to let your annuals establish well.

Hopefully, it should go without saying that you should avoid tinkering with any form of weedkiller or chemicals. Most meadow wildflowers are weeds!

The chances are that the first year might be slightly disappointing, but do persevere. A good meadow needs a few years to get established and look stunning. And don't forget, just because it's a wildflower meadow does not mean you cannot tinker with it. You can grow seeds in the pot and add them, while if there is something growing that you take a dislike to, you can remove it. It might be a wildflower meadow, but it isn't wild.

VISITING A NATURE RESERVE

You might assume that you are treating yourself by visiting a nature reserve, or some other wildlife-rich haven. And it's true that being outdoors among nature is something that provides benefits of well-being and health, mental and physical. However, your visit can be much more than that. It will invariably be an encouragement to those who run it, because footfall is part of how they measure their success, and if you use facilities such as car parks and cafes you will bring money in.

And you can do something else, too. Bring a friend.

If we are to win the battle to conserve Britain's wildlife and wildlife places, then we have to win hearts and minds or, to put it baldly, recruits. Nobody can be won over to nature if they don't experience nature. So at this moment, in the 2020s, we are going to need a sea-change in the countryside, a massive turnout of people coming to enjoy wild(ish) places who haven't done so before. It might be messy, literally in some cases (see 'Litter Picking', page 207), but our natural world is at stake.

Obviously, recruiting children is helpful, and we need many more to come visiting nature reserves, including school parties. But we need everybody else too. We need mums to come to safe places with their peers and children, people to drop in after work, people coming from the city to get fresh air. The list goes on. We need them all.

We need decision makers to come. If I could invent one law, it would be that nobody could enter the House of Commons as an MP unless they had spent at least two or three days in wild Britain, tutored in wildlife by one of our countrywide army of enthusiasts – just for fun, not to badger them or influence them. Some would slip through the net, but others could have their perceptions profoundly changed. We need councillors, business leaders, faith group leaders and more, all to come and see what is out there.

It has also been mooted recently that there should be a National Nature Service, situated somewhere between the National Health Service and National Service. Instead of staying at home, some people could instead be employed looking after our wild places, receiving fresh air for their own health and boosting conservation in Britain. It would cost the government peanuts and potentially introduce thousands of people to nature, many of whom might not connect otherwise.

Anyway, if you are visiting a nature reserve with a friend, colleague, your own children or borrowed children, here are a few suggestions.

- Make sure there is something cool to see. If possible, ensure there is a 'wow' moment. Maybe you can find a good perch for a kingfisher or visit a starling murmuration. It's easier to delight kids with bugs from ponds and so on, but adults need something else for their attention.
- Don't expect children to be quiet. When they visit, they need to have fun, so don't hush them. Okay, you might enter a hide and flush all the birds away, but the important thing is to get the kids out there.
- Don't expect anyone to be quiet. Talk normally.
- Dress comfortably. Make sure you and your visitors are warm enough (you often have to wait to see wildlife). Insist they can wear normal clothes – maybe not high heels, but people should be dissuaded from the notion that there is a uniform that outdoor people wear.
- Most adults will appreciate an attached cafe. On some reserves (for example, the London Wetland Centre), more people visit the restaurant than the hides, which is fine.
- Don't take too long.

- Use a nature reserve for social events.

One other thing that should be mentioned about nature reserves. The staff love to run events showcasing the area, and they will be encouraged by every person that enrols. If they do that, do consider joining in and, of course, you have an extra reason to bring that friend. Also, why not suggest things that you or your friends or family might enjoy – a dawn chorus, for example?

CITIZEN SCIENCE AND OBSERVATIONS

If you have read some of the individual species sections in this book, you might have noticed that, for a remarkable number of them, contributing your sightings to relevant interest groups is extremely important. Those animals include stag beetles, eels, swifts and basking sharks.

One of the biggest contributions a single person or household can make to help wildlife is by submitting observations. *This is really important.*

Here are some that you can get involved with. Be warned – this is a whole new and addictive way of life.

RSPB BIG GARDEN BIRDWATCH

Everybody should join the biggest citizen science project in the world. It takes place in the final weekend in January. Watch your garden for an hour and record the maximum numbers of each garden bird species seen at any one time. Easy to enter, good fun at a dull time of year. Schools can enter, too. Full details are available on the RSPB website.

BTO GARDEN BIRDWATCH

This is the upgraded version of the Big Garden Birdwatch and is run by the British Trust for Ornithology. It requires more commitment than the hour a year of the Big Garden Birdwatch, but provides scientists and policymakers with a lot more information. Instead, you list the birds using your garden every week, and if you wish to you can record other wildlife too, which is very helpful. You send in a list each week with highest numbers. More information is on the British Trust for Ornithology website.

BEEWALK

BeeWalk is a national recording scheme to monitor the abundance of bumblebees across the UK. To quote from their website, it involves 'volunteer "BeeWalkers" walking the same fixed route (transect) once a month between March and October, counting the bumblebees seen and identifying them to species and caste (queen, worker, male) where possible'. This doesn't sound like a bad thing to do on a sunny afternoon. Your site can be anywhere, not just in a bee-rich meadow. For more information see the Bumblebee Conservation website.

MAMMAL MAPPER

This morning, before writing this section I saw a weasel scampering across the road as I was driving my son to get a haircut. This is precisely the sort of random observation that can go into the Mammal Society's Mammal Mapper app. The free app enables you to run up a list of mammals you have seen in all the places you go, or simply add a single observation. Every record is vital in monitoring our mammal populations.

BIG BUTTERFLY COUNT

Now you really don't want to upset the great Sir David Attenborough, do you? Thought not. So, you'd better join him and thousands of others taking part in the Big Butterfly Count every year. It's hardly a burden. You simply choose a sunny day during the assigned period (which might vary from year to year) and spend 15 minutes recording what you see. Record the maximum number of each you see (the total number during a walk, or the most you can see at a time if watching from your garden at another fixed point). And then record it online.

MOTHS COUNT

As with the above, this is run by the admirable organisation, Butterfly Conservation. It is run in conjunction with the National Moth Recording Scheme. As mentioned on page 138, moths are simply awesome, and this scheme will help you get into them.

NATIONAL AMPHIBIAN AND REPTILE RECORDING SCHEME

Well, there had to be one, didn't there? If anything, records of these animals are even more precious than usual, since there is so little information out there on how they are faring. There is more information on the Amphibian and Reptile Conservation (ARC) website.

OTHER CITIZEN SCIENCE AND VOLUNTEER PROGRAMMES

The charity MARINElife want to hear about observations of sea mammals such as dolphins. They also train people to do sea transects.

The Marine Conservation Society wants to hear about basking shark sightings, as well as others such as sea turtles, jellyfish and crawfish (not crayfish).

People's Trust for Endangered Species cannot wait for your submissions to the Great Stag Hunt. They even run Stag Weekends – great stuff!

They are also interested in water voles, dormice, hedgehogs and much else. They are a great organisation that punches above its weight.

If you are keen on eels, have a look at the website of the Zoological Society of London.

UNCONVENTIONAL GARDENING

Not everyone's home comes with a garden attached. But don't despair. You can still be a gardener, even if it is a guerrilla gardener. There is still much that you can offer to your neighbourhood. Here are a few ideas.

ALLOTMENTS

If you don't have a garden, consider acquiring an allotment. These are pockets of land available for rent on which to grow flowers or fruit and vegetables. You cannot simply let them run wild; you must abide by the rules. Allotments can be incredibly productive, growing more food per square metre than prime farmland or orchards.

WINDOW BOX GARDENING

At the other end of the allotment in size is the window box. Some gardeners might look down on this micro-gardening, but bees, butterflies and moths aren't laughing. In an urban area, it can be just what they need. Most people put containers on their windowsill or patio, but pots are good if you have a little more room. Plastic containers are the lightest and best; please use peat-free compost. If you have no room at all, see if you can fix a light container onto the exterior wall (ask permission if you rent).

Many people grow vegetables or succulents in their boxes, but the wildlife gardener has an easier task. Just grow flowers — a mix of lavender, salvia and thyme, for example.

COMMUNITY GARDENS

Not everybody has a garden, but most people have access to some kind of community space. These spaces are not always managed for wildlife, but there is no reason why they shouldn't be! In fact, the Royal Botanic Gardens, Kew runs a national scheme called Grow Wild which provides advice on how to grow wildlife-friendly plants from seed. One of the scheme's sponsors is the National Lottery Community Fund. Since 2013, four million people have taken part in transforming spaces, most of them urban. However, you don't need to live in a city; any community space will do.

DOING THE COUNCIL'S JOB

Local authorities are tasked with looking after road verges and other municipal spaces, including parks. To be honest, they sometimes make a horrible mess of it, spraying when there is no need, for example, and mowing wildflower havens. If you keep finding yourself seeing red at the lack of care for wildlife, you can do something about it – after all, councils are elected to serve people like us. Try to contact somebody in the council, usually under the heading 'Parks', 'Biodiversity' or 'Environment'.

The first step is often to highlight what problems you see. Be diplomatic. Many councils may simply be ignorant of what wildlife needs, and also of what wildlife-minded people want, so approach them respectfully. If you can get some extra local support, so much the better. Most people are blissfully unaware how a few positive decisions can do wonders for wildlife in the local area, including council members.

Secondly, if you are ambitious and have the time and energy, expect to be part of the solution. Local authorities are always grateful for volunteers (see 'Litter Picking', page 207) and this can include people willing to take responsibility for the management of an open space. In these cases, everybody wins: you get the issue off your chest, the council saves money and the wildlife rocks. See the Bumblebee Conservation Trust's excellent pack for more information.

LIVING CHURCHYARDS AND ECOCHURCH

Churchyards can be fantastic places for wildlife, and they are usually looked after by volunteers. Why not volunteer to help? The Church of England's Living Churchyard Project has been taken up by numerous parishes countrywide. On a broader front, churches can also enrol for Eco Church, in which various badges are awarded for environmentally friendly heating, lighting and much else. It is run by the admirable A Rocha International charity that mobilises Christians to care about the living world.

SCHOOL GARDENING

Many school grounds contain small parcels of land which could be used to create a wildlife garden, or even tiny surfaces for pots and window boxes. This is especially important if children don't normally have opportunities to take part in gardening themselves or to see bees, hoverflies and butterflies buzzing towards flowers that they themselves have potted. It is a thrill to see animals enjoying the fruits of your work. The Royal Horticultural Society has an excellent resource pack and offers training courses.

GUERRILLA GARDENING

This term describes gardening on land to which you have no legal right. It sounds dodgy, but it is usually done to fill spaces that seem to be abandoned or neglected. In London, for example, people sometimes just plant attractive flowers in rundown corners; others actually grow fruit and vegetables. There is a website called Guerrilla Gardening.

There is an aspect of protest in guerrilla gardening. Many public authorities have reduced green space, and this planting can be seen as retribution. Some people have thrown 'seed bombs' on to amenity spaces. However, unless you are naturally rebellious, why not contact your local authority to find out whether you are breaking any byelaws.

LITTER PICKING AND BEACH CLEANING

The nuisance of litter is something that many people find annoying. It spoils the look of places and is sometimes harmful. The thing that makes ordinary people see red is that it is also completely unnecessary. People can and should clear up after their activities, but for some reason a lot of people seem to be too lazy and antisocial to do so. Across Britain, £1 billion a year is spent on the clean-up, potentially useful funds down the drain.

So, beauty spots are strewn with cans, plastic bags and worse. The tideline on beaches takes on the appearance of a tip. People throw unwanted items out of their cars while driving, leaving verges stained.

But while Britain's citizens fume, wildlife suffers. For us it's an eyesore, for an animal it can be literally sore. Litter kills and maims. Litter can sentence an animal to an agonising death. Many of us have seen the plastic can-holders that have caught around the neck of a swan, or the plastic bags eaten by sea turtles until they choke, and birds that have been injured by the sharp sides of cans.

The irony is that some people who leave rubbish in the countryside love dogs and cats. They might like tweets about dolphins and seals. They might watch TV programmes about sharks or pandas. They would do anything for their children, yet in another moment might leave a broken bottle in a car park for somebody else's child to step on. They are you and me in moments of carelessness and ignorance. On the other hand, other people couldn't care less.

We can't change society, but we can at least do something about this ourselves, and that is to volunteer to help pick it up. It is not the most glamorous conservation work ever devised, but it is very important. There are serious brownie points to be gained here. Here are some suggestions for getting involved in clearing up litter.

BEACH CLEANING

This is the ultimate dirty weekend and a lot of people do it. It is an excellent family day out – honestly. If you take children on a beach clean, they are certain to have a good time and you have the extra bonus that they will learn about keeping the environment clean. In surveys, almost everyone who has attended an event is more likely to be more careful with their subsequent use of plastic and more assiduous with their recycling.

In a normal year there is a beach clean somewhere almost every weekend. Remarkably, Beachwatch, which is organised by the Marine Conservation Society, has almost 900 organisers. A wide tract of Britain's coastline is covered, and their website even has a map showing the gaps that need to be filled in. There are other agencies doing similar good work, including the National Trust and Surfers Against Sewage.

To get you started, you could join in with the Great British Beach Clean, which takes place every September. In 2019 there were 437 events, with 10,800 volunteers taking part. They removed 10,833kg of litter, which is almost 11 tonnes in all. Not bad for a single weekend. You might conclude that this is a drop in the ocean, so to speak, but scientific studies have shown that this level of beach cleaning significantly affects a beach's cleanliness for quite some time afterwards.

And let's face it, it is badly needed. The litter on beaches is doubly problematic because it doesn't only degrade the beach habitat itself (and may deter tourists visiting as well as harming beach wildlife), but much of what is left on beaches, for example by day trippers, will eventually end up in the sea itself. And we all know what happens then. One third of the world seabird species, 26 marine mammals and almost all the world's sea turtles have been damaged by ingesting debris. Animals get entangled in plastic and fishing line – indeed, discarded fishing gear is a major problem worldwide. Much human rubbish is also toxic when ingested by sea creatures. Plastics are especially pernicious because they take hundreds of years to degrade, physically breaking down into micro-plastics (less than 5mm in size), and the impact of these particles is still being investigated. Micro-plastics are known to get into the intestinal tracts of larger marine organisms, blocking them up and causing starvation. Their impact on people is not yet known; they are hardly likely to do us much good.

Knowing all this, no wonder so many people get involved in beach cleans. You only need attend for a couple of hours. You are given protective clothing and you use a long-handled litter-picker, so you don't normally touch every item you find – you really wouldn't want to! At many events prior to the pandemic year of 2020, there would often be 100–200 at a beach-cleaning event. Many people who attended once came back again for more!

And why not organise your own? The sense of achievement, if nothing else, makes it worthwhile.

LITTER PICKING INLAND

This is the less glamorous end of litter picking. Somehow, the atmosphere of a beach negates some of the ghastliness of the activity, whereas this might not be the case inland. Nevertheless, it is just as important. Just remember that every piece of litter taken is a potential life saved.

The equivalent to the Great British Beach clean on land is World Clean-up Day, which seeks to pick up litter in every kind of environment in many countries throughout the world. This might be a place to start.

However, all over the country volunteers are needed. Keep Britain Tidy is the admirable charity that keep much of this going. It works with local authorities and runs campaigns to keep parks free of litter, for example. They also hand out awards for park (Green Flag Award) and for towns and cities (Keep Britain Tidy Awards).

The more you look, the more you will find that people are dedicating time to this cause. Why not enquire at your local nature reserve and see if they have teams doing this?

CAMPAIGNS TO JOIN
(OR HOW TO ANNOY A CONSERVATIONIST)

A few months back I put out a Twitter request to ask wildlife enthusiasts which matters in the countryside most riled them. The replies were abundant, varied and often fruity. Clearly, certain things really get to people. They are usually stupid things that, with a little effort, should be avoided, such as unnecessary spraying of verges. Some are those nasty little habits that developers get up to, and others are money-making schemes that potentially do harm to the countryside. Many are just people not knowing.

Here is a list of the main ones. Do consider any campaigns that might make the relevant people aware of these problems.

SPRAYING VERGES

Councils and keepers, ladies and gentlemen, this is the *number one* irritation for conservation-minded voters. We absolutely hate it when you spray, trim or mow verges for no reason other than wanting to keep them 'tidy'. If there is no obvious hazard, such as visibility to traffic, there is no point in doing this. Verges are biodiversity hotspots and should be cherished. It costs money to pay somebody to ruin good wildlife habitat when you could be paying many more people to promote the environment.

The culture of municipal tidiness is a relatively modern fad that has no place in the climate crisis. Stop doing it. As one of the wildlife Twitterati said: 'Lots of the changes needed to help wildlife are hard to do, but doing less mowing and other cutting is not one of them.'

Good verges are true wildlife havens. Take flowers. No less than 700 species of native flowering plants have been discovered and recorded on road verges, which is about half the total across the whole country. And that's without taking into account all the other treasures.

PLASTIC LAWNS

It is quite faddish at the moment to replace those troublesome grassy bits in your garden with gleaming AstroTurf. It will look neat and tidy, even at the edges. You can even hoover up any horrible things like leaves, that's if you don't have plastic leaves and plastic flowers. Your garden will need less attention, which means you can spend more time on your smartphone and going shopping. What's not to like?

Well, everything, really. I understand that there is an attraction to low-maintenance gardens for the infirm who can no longer manage, but the rest of us? Do me a favour.

For a start, gardening is good for you and your mental health, whereas looking after plastic isn't. It's essentially the same as housework. Secondly, plastic lawns don't last forever and need to be removed; very few can ever be recycled, so they become yet more plastic waste. Thirdly, in very hot weather, which our country is seeing more and more of these days, it can get uncomfortable to stand on them.

But the worst thing about a plastic lawn is its intrinsic wildlife value, which is nil. In fact, it causes harm by blocking leaf litter and humus reaching the soil and replenishing it. Grasses cannot grow, lawn weeds such as clover cannot come up. Worms can't reach the surface. Robins and blackbirds can't reach the worms that can't reach the surface.

Kids in these sorts of gardens miss out on the feeling of grass on their toes, or the thrill of wiggly worms, or mud and puddles. They miss out on the smell of rain on grass, or the scent of a mown lawn. They miss out on the beauty of imperfection outdoors, the unpredictability of what lies between the glass blades, the thrill of putting your finger in the dirt.

What kind of world do we want? As you will realise from other parts of this book, gardens are where conservationists can start mending our country. Every garden with a plastic lawn is a step backwards.

There are some people, such as Dave Goulson, author of *The Garden Jungle*, who think they should be banned. Join the campaign.

NETTING OVER TREES

Building developers sometimes pretend that they care about wildlife, but they don't really, and especially not when it gets in the way of making money. One of their excruciating ruses in recent years has been to put up netting to prevent birds nesting in trees on land that they have earmarked for development. This is sometimes done to get planning permission, arguing that birds are not nesting there. It is also sometimes done to ensure that, when they build, they can't be accused of disturbing birds in the breeding season.

DOG POO HUNG UP ON BUSHES

In the pantheon of littering offences, this has to be the strangest. Honestly, what induces people to go to the trouble of removing their dog's poop into a bag, then hanging it up as if it's some kind of trophy? Apparently, it is occasionally said to be a protest about not providing enough dog litter bins. So how does that work? You hang up your potty bags, sometimes within the reach of children, and then people will automatically get the message that there aren't enough bins? Yeah, right. There are ways to ask for more bins, and that's to ask the appropriate people to provide more bins.

Apart from this ignoble 'cause', why do people do it? It's simple really. They cannot be bothered to dispose of their dog's mess because they are too lazy and arrogant. They think that if the bag is hung in plain sight, somebody will come and deal with it. What a fun job that is – thank you, dog owner. Their attitude is even worse than that. They originally put the mess in the bag because of peer pressure, thinking perhaps that they might be spotted. Then, when the coast is clear, they dispose of the evidence. What's wrong with these people?

It so happens that doing this is illegal. Fines range from £50 to £80. If you are one of these people, we hate you – but please at least use biodegradable bags!

BIRD SPIKES

Some institutions have recently got into the habit of placing spikes where birds often perch – for example, to roost – in order to prevent bird poo falling 'in the wrong place'. There was a recent case of a fire station doing worse than this – they cut down trees used by starlings as a roost, just to protect their fire engines being pooed upon. Why couldn't they have just cleaned it up? It isn't as if they don't have enough hoses!

FLY-TIPPING

This is a particular pernicious form of littering, because it is not only illegal but is mainly done by professional tradespersons trying to avoid charges, which means that it usually involves large items. We've all seen sofas, chairs, mattresses and the like dumped in quiet corners by the roadside. Just before writing this I found what looked like a pile of garden waste, but it was piled over a pushchair that somebody had just got rid of, a deliberate attempt at concealment.

Fly-tipping can't be excused by ignorance or sob-stories. It's just wrong. And it costs taxpayers money. In 2016/17 more than *a million* incidents were dealt with in England alone, to a cost to you and me of £58 million.

If you see it in action, try to get details, but bearing in mind it is illegal, don't confront or approach the offenders. Report it to your local council or the Environment Agency.

COMPOST MADE FROM PEAT

I have mentioned this in some other sections but repeat it here because *there is no reason why you need peat compost and it should not be sold at all.*

The problem is twofold. Peat must be sourced from somewhere, and the peat bogs of Britain are often fabulous natural habitats in their own right, habitats where lots of uncommon birds such as waders nest. Digging them for peat means no birds. Now that Britain's supplies are running out, rapacious companies are sourcing peat from abroad, doing just as much damage.

Secondly, our peat bogs hold vast amounts of carbon dioxide, which is released when they are disturbed. British bogs have sequestered about 5.5 billion tonnes of carbon, and worldwide half a trillion tonnes, more than in all the world's forests. As peat is removed from its inundated state in the ground, it eventually gives off all its carbon dioxide, whether in transit or in your garden; in the natural habitat, carbon continues to be lost.

Using natural peat in compost, ruining the habitat and releasing carbon is simply scandalous. It is incredible how many garden centres and supermarkets sell peat compost. Many famous gardeners, such as Monty Don from *Gardeners' World*, are dead set against it. Yet retailers still sell it.

Make a fuss. Drive them crazy. Campaign. End this madness.

DISPOSABLE BARBECUES

We have all seen these being sold in the supermarket and perhaps used them in our gardens. It might be said that they don't fit so well in the countryside, though.

This is for two reasons. The first and most obvious is that they cause fires. It is easy to have your picnic and leave the barbecue in situ without putting it out, usually just by mistake. In tinder-dry country this is predictably disastrous.

As several correspondents pointed out, the problem is that word, 'disposable'. This almost makes it acceptable for people just to leave their barbecue behind, littering the ground. The reality is that, if you're having an outdoor barbecue, they are quite awkward to dispose of.

An outright ban would help the environment. Don't get your hopes up.

LITTERING

Litter isn't just a problem, it's a question of psychology.

As mentioned elsewhere, there is no reason why people should leave litter intentionally in the countryside, but it happens. In recent years, the issue seems to have upgraded somewhat into a crisis of education and attitude. Now people leave tents and sleeping bags behind them after 'wild camping', along with the rest of their trash. Many of these habits seem to have become engrained during music festivals, when leaving behind your stuff seems to be the norm.

The really strange thing about this is that the same people who litter the countryside probably insist on their own house interiors being clean and tidy. Perhaps they have perfect gardens too. Yet when they go to the countryside, they seem to think it is somebody else's job to clean up after them, as if they were at a party.

Personally, I would love to see the government impose a tax on items such as tents and barbecues that are regularly dumped outdoors. Then they might become prohibitively expensive. It won't happen, of course. Making money is everything, apparently.

HEDGE FLAILING AND DESTRUCTION

Many in the rural communities, farmers and conservationists alike, have understood for decades how important hedges are. Whether used as boundaries for fields, or in the garden, they are fantastic resources for wildlife. Yet they are often abused. Gardeners and council workers may cut them during the breeding season, for no other reason than to make them look 'tidy'. This is a pointless conceit that is environmentally damaging.

And talking of that, hedges are often flailed by machines on farms on an annual basis. This has the effect of opening up the hedge and often stopping the hedge shrubs flowering in a given year. Although hedges are quite difficult to look after without spending a lot of money, this well-known destruction needs to be halted.

Even today, some farmers grub out hedgerows. In many cases this is now illegal, and always when the hedgerow is more than 30 years old or more than 20m long, and they need special permission to do it. Farmers must not work on hedgerows when the birds are nesting between 1 March and 31 August. But these rules are sometimes flouted.

PLASTIC FOUR-PACK RINGS FOR DRINKS

These are awful in every way and should be banned. Quite apart from being useless, they often harm wildlife.

WEEDKILLERS

Conservationists aren't keen on weedkillers. This is hardly surprising, since the very definition of a 'weed' is a 'plant in the wrong place'. It doesn't refer to specific plants, just ones that somebody has taken a dislike to, and that's a matter of opinion. Weedkillers kill many very attractive native plants and are a blunt instrument. They are overused, in farming, gardening and in treating verges and parks.

The most successful weedkiller is glyphosate, better known by its trade name Roundup. It is used everywhere. In a recent German study, 99% of people surveyed had this weedkiller in their urine. Surely this cannot be a good thing.

Weedkillers can be useful, but nobody knowns what long-term effects they might have on people. They certainly aren't kind to plants. These chemicals are literally everywhere, and we don't know anything like enough about them. What problems are we storing up for ourselves?

NIGHT-TIME LIGHTING

Night-time lighting in this country is excessive. It is also incredibly expensive and bad for the environment to keep lights on, especially in office blocks where nobody is working and in shops where nobody can go in. It is understandable to be fearful of crime, and there is a health and safety aspect, but at what stage do we decide that there is too much?

In cities, the dawn chorus happens earlier because of street and other lighting. Robins sometimes sing all night. Bats are more susceptible to predation in artificial light. In the migration season, birds are often attracted to the lights of high-rise buildings, and many are killed or disoriented. Who knows how many moths are lured in to artificial lights, perhaps also to be killed?

LACK OF EDUCATION

Why is there so little education on the environment, particularly in secondary schools? We frighten our children to death with warnings and fears of climate change, but we should also show them the majesty and fascination of the natural world. This subject used to be on the curriculum, and there are plans afoot for a new natural history GCSE, but why isn't there one already? We won't persuade children to look after the natural world unless they love it. Add your voice by writing to your MP (see page 231) or to the Department for Education.

TACKLING WILDLIFE CRIME

Wildlife crime is crime enshrined in law, and many environmental protections are also enshrined in law. But how much money goes into tackling wildlife crime and enforcement? Peanuts, of course. The penalties imposed are often nominal, so that at the end of a trial it feels hardly worthwhile. This happens in every area of environment – illegal shooting and trapping, pollution incidents by water companies, breaching of tree protection orders, development without planning permission, littering, dog fouling and many others.

ENGINES RUNNING UNNECESSARILY

Hello, car owners. Did you know it is illegal to leave your engine running by the side of a public road? At present, you can get a fine of £20.

BALLOONS AND OTHER RELEASES

Helium balloons are a disaster for the environment. The sad thing is that they are often released in commemoration of a loved one, or a poignant and special event, and nobody doubts that they can be dramatic and meaningful. The saddest thing of all is that, after the emotional high of a release, balloons can cause misery for animals and for the environment, and sometimes death.

The harm of balloons released in large numbers is manifold. Although some balloon companies claim that latex balloons are biodegradable, there doesn't seem to be any evidence for that. And besides, they can choke a turtle to death long before they degrade. See the Balloons Blow website for information and alternatives.

CHINESE LANTERNS

Chinese lanterns and other sky lanterns fall into the same category as balloons. There is no doubt they look beautiful upon release, but unfortunately, once they have blown away, they cause potential harm to animals. Surely nobody, except maybe hard-nosed businesses selling them, would wish to cause great suffering to an animal entangled in a fallen lantern or injured by the wire frame. This is what sometimes happens, though. The ornaments are also a fire risk and, in common with balloons, never as biodegradable as claimed.

Chinese lanterns have been banned in Wales on council land since 2018, and groups such as the Royal Society for the Prevention of Cruelty to Animals (RSPCA) are lobbying hard for a countrywide ban.

ABANDONED FISHING TACKLE

This has been a problem for years, yet it never seems to get any better. The trouble is that discarded fishing line, hooks and nets are all genuine hazards for wildlife. The problem affects not just inland waterways, but even more the marine environment.

LEAF BLOWERS

The leaf blower should have been strangled at birth. Whatever was wrong with a rake and a little healthy work? Leaf blowers are designed for what exactly? OK, for blowing leaves from one place to another, usually in the name of 'tidiness'. What a pointless exercise. Yes, leaves do fall on paths and mulch and get slippery and somebody might fall over but put a sign up warning people. And what's wrong with fallen leaves? They don't damage your lawn; in fact, they are good food for your precious earthworms. You can simply add piles of leaves to your compost heap.

Leaf blowers are noisy, emit noxious fumes and can injure people and pets by blowing leaves into their eyes. Autumn, with its falling leaves, has been going on and off since the Cretaceous, so maybe 70 million years. We evolved maybe 100,000 years ago and, weirdly, we don't seem to have needed leaf-blowers before now.

HS2

Who knows, by the time you read this, the fuss over this high speed rail link might have subsided. Or it might yet have been cancelled. Oddly, for what is a broadly green project, conservationists and activists just hate everything about it.

Why? It cuts through irreplaceable ancient woodlands and will affect many nature reserves. The route looks to have been designed to go through 'soft' targets rather than housing or farmland. The company running it are arrogant, ignorant and many of their employees wildly overpaid.

Perhaps more than anything, HS2 irritates us because it is the ultimate example of low-hanging fruit that, in its cancellation, might have placated conservationists. It is wildly over-budget, desperately unpopular for many in the shires and, particularly now that so few people are commuting, will almost certainly never fulfil the role for which it was designed.

If a government cannot kill off such a project, what will they ever do that might even be mildly difficult for the cause of conservation?

RESPONSIBLE PET OWNERSHIP

The popularity of pets has boomed in recent years. And, in common with many a trend that seems largely benign, it has its downside. Everybody who visits their local beauty spot and sees small black bags hung on trees or gateposts, a little reminder of their pet's poop, will know this well.

You might be shocked, though, about just how bad our pets can be when it comes to interactions with our native wildlife. If you don't wish to know, I suggest you look away now.

Of course, I understand there are many good things about cats and dogs. They are good company and help people get out and about and keep people healthy, especially their mental health. I say this to get out alive after you have read the rest.

The trouble is that both dogs and cats are predators and cats, in particular, have an independent streak. When the cat's away, it plays. If left unsupervised, it will do what cats do: kill stuff. A survey from 1997 estimated that the UK's cats killed about five million reptiles and amphibians in a year.

Think that's bad? A more recent survey by the Mammal Society reckoned that the nine million cats in this country kill 27 million birds every year, and 100 million animals altogether if you take into account rodents such as rats and mice. Their top bird casualties are house sparrows, starlings, blue tits and blackbirds. These 100 million are only during the summer, and the estimate only takes into account reported killings. There may be more that the cats left behind, or simply injured. 100 million casualties adds up to 11,000 a day. This, by any account, is a massive slaughter.

As for dogs, you might think that they are less destructive to wildlife. However, they can also cause a great deal of harm when left off a lead. They routinely run after wildlife and are a particular hazard during the breeding season, when they flush ground-nesting birds. Dogs frequently attack several animals in this book, including stag beetles, hedgehogs, adders and red squirrels. During the winter they often flush roosting birds, such as waders, next to estuaries and on beaches; indeed, owners sometimes positively encourage them to do so. The owners are presumably unaware that constant disturbance can cause birds to starve and die.

But how much harm do they really do? The answer to this is shocking. A study from the Humber Estuary found that dogs off the lead caused more disruption than any other activity except for fighter jets flying overhead, and another from New Zealand produced the same surprising result, that dog walking caused more disruption than any other leisure activity. Another study from woodland trails in New South Wales, Australia, found that dog walking produced a 35% reduction in species richness compared to control locations with no dogs, and 41% fewer individual birds were seen. These reductions were twice those measured with humans walking alone. On small reserves up to 40% of species stay away of dogs are present. These are extraordinary and alarming findings.

And that's without the poo. As you'll see from page 213, this is a huge issue for all other users of green space, especially when it is left in non-disposable bags and hung on trees or bushes. On a reserve in Lincolnshire, volunteers found 75 faeces on the ground along 180m of footpath which led to a car park fitted with dog bins and even a dog lavatory. Dog faeces is naturally unpleasant, smelly and can be hazardous.

With at least 1.5 billion dog walks in the UK each year, and with 9.9 million pet dogs around, the problems won't go away. However, it is also abundantly clear from the figures that most dog owners are responsible. Most have little idea of any damage they are causing. Furthermore, dog walking is a healthy and life-giving pursuit.

As ever, compromise is required. From my own experience I know that dog owners don't like being reminded if they are breaking a rule, but they should be far more amenable to this. Equally, banning dogs to preserve wildlife could set people against wildlife conservation.

Here, though, are a few tips for cat and dog owners:

Cats

- Keep your cat indoors at night.
- Fit your cat with a bell to warn potential prey.

Dogs

- Please respect signs asking for leads or close control.
- Don't allow your dog to chase flocks of birds.
- Don't allow your dog to get out of control.
- Clear up poo and dispose of it appropriately.
- Don't get huffy when somebody asks you to do the above, especially if it is a staff member or volunteer from a nature reserve.

FEEDING GARDEN BIRDS

Feeding garden birds is one of conservation's no-brainers. You put up a bird feeder, the local birds come to tuck in, and you get to enjoy their antics. What isn't to like?

At first, you might not think garden bird feeding is of conservation value. The birds, however, disagree. Several species have expanded their natural ranges or migratory habits because of widespread provision by kind-hearted householders. For example, most British goldfinches used to leave the country in the winter; now they slum it in our gardens. Blackcaps used to be rare in Britain in the winter; now birds from Central Europe have changed their migration to winter here instead of Spain, mainly because of garden feeding. The siskin, once mainly a bird of large conifer forests, is now a frequent garden visitor, and is expanding in southern England. Gardens also act as a refuge from our desolate farmlands for hedgerow birds such as bullfinches and yellowhammers, attracted to a land of plenty. British gardens cover more land than all our National Nature Reserves put together, so if every garden was a one-stop shop for birds, the benefits would be enormous.

And it isn't just the birds that are nourished; so are people. People love watching the comings and goings at feeders. It is good for our well-being, whether we are young or old. Many care homes have found how important it is to provide this inexpensive entertainment, especially for those residents who have limited mobility. Birds in the garden are a reminder of nature, and nature is the best and cheapest escape from the stresses of life.

And feeding birds is so easy to do; you simply put up some kind of dispenser, whether it's a simple tray or a multi-perch hanging feeder of the type you can buy from the RSPB or a garden centre. The birds aren't interested in the design. It takes very little to make them visit.

These days, we have learnt a great deal about how best to provide for birds, and the rule is that regularity, hygiene and nutrition are all worth considering. Regularity simply means that you put out foods dependably; birds are creatures of habit and greatly appreciate it if you keep re-stocking so that they find food when they need it (especially in the short, cold days of deep winter). Hygiene is necessary to prevent disease spreading. If possible, wash your feeder or table-top every couple of weeks in warm, soapy water. Also, try to move feeders to prevent accumulation of waste below, which might otherwise attract unwanted rodents. It is also a good idea to use no-mess seed mixtures.

As far as nutrition is concerned, we now know that certain foods are better for birds. Once upon a time, everybody put out scraps, including bread and raisins. Now, though, bread is somewhat frowned upon in the same way that you are discouraged from feeding fast food to your children. Instead, a whole industry has now arisen that enables you to serve up five-star foods for your birds. Certain foodstuffs are prescribed for different visitors. Although expensive, this is great. You can also use different types of feeders for different birds. There are also squirrel-proof feeders.

People are often dismayed when their carefully assembled bird restaurants attract more than they bargained for, with predators such as sparrowhawks visiting to eat their customers. Don't worry about this, it's nature. If you have a sparrowhawk it's a sign of a healthy bird population; you could consider the predator as a Michelin star. It won't kill all your birds, I promise.

Some people have advised against feeding birds in the summer. Ignore this. The reasons put forward were that parent birds might give their nestlings inappropriate food. Many years ago, some baby birds were found choked to death on peanuts. However, this will only have happened in time of extreme food shortage, when the adults simply couldn't find the right food, and went with what they could. Think about it: parent birds are programmed to feed the right food to their young, otherwise the species would die out. So don't worry, in normal conditions the parent birds will probably use your feeders as an easy food supply to support them when they are looking for the correct food for their young.

I have heard it said that, by feeding birds artificially, we are producing lazy individuals and that, somehow, second-rate birds are being brought forth from the garden environment. This might have some truth if it weren't for the fact that very few birds would ever spend all year using artificial food supplies; the rest of the time they will be wandering. This is really not something that you need to lie awake worrying about. What might give you sleepless nights is your budget. You don't really need to feed birds in summer, and most especially not in autumn, when few birds use the garden anyway. Ideally, feed them most from December onwards.

March and April are critical times to feed birds. These are the difficult months when the stocks of seeds and nuts in the wild are running out, and before the insect flush has set in. This is when your birds need you.

When we talk about feeding birds in our gardens, we might overlook the fact that there are two main ways of doing this. Yes, we can place food into feeders, but just as important is to plant bird-friendly herbage, particularly berry-bearing shrubs. Ivy, a plant with a fraught relationship with gardeners, is an absolute must because it bears berries at an unusual time. Berries also look great, so that is an additional benefit. There is a list of good berry-bearing shrubs and other good bird plants on the website of BBC's *Gardeners' World*.

SUPPORT REWILDING

Rewilding – it's a buzz word at the moment and it means a lot of things. But at heart it involves redirecting land towards management for the benefit of nature.

Everyone should be excited by rewilding. If conservation was reimagined as a football match, conservationists have been fighting a defensive, backs-to-the-wall game against governments, planners, landowners and developers for decades. Rewilding is the thrilling breakaway, working deep into our opponent's half and scoring the unexpected winning goal. Rewilding is powerful, joyous, optimistic. Sensible rewilding is the future.

Some people make the mistake that rewilding is simply to remove all management from a site and let nature take its course. As an overall plan of action, this rarely works. More typically, a rewilding scheme will require planning and a great deal of effort, as well as any relevant permissions. The British countryside is so far from its natural state that, apart from some parts of Scotland, for instance, it won't be of much use if left to its own devices.

Another fallacy about rewilding is that it's all about wildlife, but every scheme has to take people into account, both locals and potential visitors. This, in some ways, is the reason that rewilding is so exciting. If you own land, most people can grasp that making money from it is reasonable. The wonderful thing about most rewilding schemes is that they can and should benefit everybody.

Benedict Macdonald in his wonderful book *Rebirding* gives the example of Scottish deer-hunting estates. At the moment, there are far too many deer in Scotland, and much the same situation applies to the rest of the country. As a result of competition, and also as a result of being left out on open moors because of deforestation, the red deer are generally in poor condition and, frankly, too easy to shoot. If you allowed the forests and scrub to grow back, the deer would have refuge. If, more controversially, you introduced perfectly natural and native predators such as lynx or wolves, the weak deer would be weeded out, the remaining deer would be supremely alert, there would be more food available and you would get far more exciting sport for visitors. Rewilding estates like this means everybody wins, economically as well as environmentally.

People are often afraid of the concept of reintroducing animals, but it has already been successful in Britain. Various schemes have had considerable success, such as the reintroduction of red kites, which now seem to be everywhere; the UK now has the highest population in the world. Ospreys have been successfully reintroduced to England and pine martens to Wales; great bustards are breeding on Salisbury Plain and storks are next. Cranes are thriving. The large blue reintroduction is a marvel. All these animals belong in Britain, and thus they are not going to get suddenly out of control and upset the balance of nature. Beavers have been shown, time and again, to be good for river ecosystems and the fish within them, despite the worries of landowners. They can also prevent flooding.

Much as it would be exciting to return lynxes, wolves and bears into southern England, it could never happen. Here rewilding is going to be less wild, but it can be every bit as valuable. Take the famous rewilding estate at Knepp Castle, in West Sussex. Surrounded by farmland and, further away, towns such as Horsham and Worthing, it might be hard to convince the nearby population that bears or wolves are a good thing. Instead, Knepp controls their grazing animals, while leaving large amounts of scrub and woodland to regenerate naturally, where nightingales and turtle doves thrive. Knepp is an example of a rewilding project that adapts to its location and neighbours, rather than the other way round. The Great Fen Project in East Anglia is the same. It embraces and inspires landowners rather than running roughshod over them and their livelihoods.

There are many rewilding projects in Britain, and they all, in their many, experimental ways, deserve your support. There is a website for Rewilding Britain which showcases what they are trying to achieve. There are projects big and small. Few involve lynxes, but they all involve dedicated people. They all need support, either by donating money or by buying their products and services, such as 'safaris'.

One of the core aims of Rewilding Britain is to 'revitalise economies in ways that work ecologically'. Nowhere is this more urgently needed than on farmland. Somehow, our farming must begin to tackle its urgent issues, such as biodiversity loss, soil erosion and depletion, and excessive use of pesticides. It is exciting that some of the 'rewilding' schemes are really 'refarming' schemes, trying to work out how ordinary agriculture can make money without impacting on the environment in adverse ways. To their credit, many farms around the country are forming their own conservation networks.

The RSPB runs Hope Farm, in Cambridgeshire, for research purposes, to see how farming and birds can mix. It builds on earlier work at Vine House farm in Lincolnshire, which suggested that what farmers really need to do to help birds is to dig ponds, plant hedges and feed birds. The work done at both may not seem to many like true 'rewilding', but it is probably in these projects that the goals of rewilding will be met.

LOBBYING

We live in a time when lobbying those in power has never been easier, or more effective. Social media is the human condition laid bare, but it can also be an agent for remarkable good. In the last few years, for example, social media campaigns have embarrassed housebuilders into removing netting designed to stop birds breeding, and councils into rethinking the cutting of verges, and there are many other examples. There is power in mobilising those of like mind. At present, any petition of any kind that obtains 10,000 signatures gets a response from the government, and any that gets 100,000 is considered for debate in parliament. We live in a democracy and, imperfect though it is, Members of Parliament (MPs) do listen to public opinion. You can get more information about creating a petition on the UK Government and Parliament website.

So powerful is social media that you can spend an afternoon doing a great deal of good. If you follow the various conservation agencies, such as the RSPB, National Trust or the Wildlife Trusts (see page 239 for details), you will easily find a cause to which you can put your signature. Even better, you can contribute to requests for money. As so often, even a small amount can be of extraordinary encouragement to a cause – protecting a local woodland or supporting a small conservation scheme. As mentioned throughout this book, it is the combination of small steps that makes things happen.

While social media is a powerful tool, do not underestimate the power of getting in contact with your local MP. If there are issues that are of importance to you, make an appointment to discuss these concerns at the local MP's surgery. MPs are compelled to be accessible and to listen to their constituents – you can write to them quickly and efficiently on the TheyWorkForYou website. The overwhelming majority of MPs are decent human beings. However, they are forever weighing up competing opinions, so it can seem frustrating at times. Yet it is truly astonishing how few people ever go to see their MP. Your time and trouble might make an important difference.

As mentioned above, MPs are human and, although they are resilient, they value common decency. One of the great modern ills of the country seems to be the inability to see a competing point of view. For example, those of us in our ecological echo chamber are 100% sure that the ongoing badger cull is wrong and the science backs us up, but that is rarely enough to convince a farmer, and the MP must weigh up both opinions.

Another vital lobbying tool is persistence. Again, MPs are human and they, like we all do, want the quietest life possible. If you are constantly bothering them with the same issue, they might be persuaded to act, especially if you keep a social media campaign going too. You need to tread the balance between persuading them and antagonising them. And MPs do change their minds sometimes.

A step down from your MP is your council. In Scotland, Wales and Northern Ireland there are 32 county councils, while in parts of England there are unitary authorities, the county, regional or metropolitan councils. Elsewhere there may be a second tier, the district, borough or city council. Amazingly, there is yet another elected tier in many places, the town, parish or community councils. It cannot be stated strongly enough that these are important positions because they all include planning matters. If local governments were full of rabid but reasonable environmentalists, mature people who realise that some battles can be won and some cannot, nature would be in less of a fix.

When it comes to lobbying, don't forget your local friends and neighbours. In this time of environmental crises, we need everybody to speak up.

One more tip for lobbying. While those in power pull the strings, there is also a class of people that have extraordinary influence and can be of great benefit to good causes – celebrities and/or influencers. Why anybody should think that it's worth listening to the opinions of a witless actor, comedian or reality 'star' is quite beyond me, but that's celebrity culture for you. The fact remains that stardust is powerful, and some good words from a *Love Island* contestant or YouTuber can be the making of a campaign. And to be fair, a few of them care a great deal about the issues. Pick carefully among the general fatuousness and witlessness, however.

YOUR MONEY

This book details dozens of ways to help save our species. But, in life, sometimes the least glamorous acts are the most effective, and the simple giving away of money to conservation charities is one of these.

A simple click of your mouse to donate to a cause is a couple of seconds' effort and a small amount of pain, but the good it can do resonates in waves beyond your imaginings.

It is annoying that conservation causes are forever short of money. Even back in 2016, it was estimated that, worldwide, $300–400 billion a year is needed to protect and restore ecosystems, but only about $52 is received annually, most from the public purse of countries, or from philanthropists. If you are reading this book and are looking to offload a few billion, this could be the cause for you. For the rest, I quote these figures not to depress or to make your contribution seem small, but simply to show the extent of the shortfall and just how important money is to the future of wildlife.

You can give money in many ways; you can also swap it for time, by giving your services as a volunteer, which amounts to the same thing.

Here are a few suggestions as to how your money can help conservation.

JOINING EXISTING ORGANISATIONS

Being a member of the RSPB and its ilk helps conservation, so you should be a member of something. Go ahead and join and, if it applies, sign a Gift Aid form and set up a direct debit. Ask for communications online.

There are a lot of organisations, many of them mentioned in this book. You cannot be a member of them all. I would recommend joining one big one (RSPB, Wildlife Trusts) and one small one (e.g. Bat Conservation Trust), the latter whatever your interest is. Then you, and your money, won't be spread too thinly.

WILLS AND LEGACIES

Nobody likes to think about dying. However, a gift given by someone departed can be of benefit for many years in the future. Don't blame organisations for asking, either. They are not being impertinent; they are doing their job.

FINANCIAL SERVICES

Some conservation organisations have agreements with banks to operate credit cards that give a cut in return. For example, the Co-operative Banking Group runs an RSPB credit card. At the time of writing, every new account opened generates £18 for the RSPB and 25p for each £100 you spend or transfer.

ADOPT A DORMOUSE, HEDGEHOG, WASP ...

Well, maybe not a wasp. But there are dozens of adoption schemes out there that give an extra bit of value to your donation because they are personal. They make good gifts, too.

CROWDFUNDING AND JUST GIVING

You don't need to look for crowdfunding ideas or other requests, they will usually come to you through social media. If they strike a chord, why not donate?

FUNDRAISING

If a conservation cause is close to your heart, why not set up your own JustGiving or

GoFundMe page, and then go and do something daft? I once spent ten days hiking in Surrey by day and catching moths at night, people sponsoring an amount per moth species. The great benefit of doing this is that everybody gains: the charity gets the money (and potential publicity), and you have a great time. You can learn a lot about yourself in the process.

VOLUNTEERING

You might be monetarily poor but time rich. If you are, charities will be falling over themselves to catch your eye. You can do as much or as little as you like but beware that you will always find yourself thinking you can do more.

Also, shop around. You are gold dust and you should be treated well and with respect.

CLIMATE CHANGE

We cannot fix climate change on our own. Neither can climate change be fixed if everyone in the UK devoted themselves to zero net emissions by changing their lives. The truth is, if the human race sorts the problem out, which is in some doubt, it will probably be done by industry and innovation. That doesn't mean, though, that moderating our lives to produce a smaller environmental impact isn't a good idea, because if widescale life changes occur along with innovation, that gives us a much better chance of saving the world. Once again, collectively we can make an enormous difference.

Many lifestyle changes we make to help the planet help us, too, allowing us to be happier and healthier. Here are just a few steps we can all make:

- Eat less meat, or none. It is astonishing how, globally, meat production is bad for the environment. A great deal of meat comes from cows, which release methane into the atmosphere. They feed on grassland, sometimes produced by clearing forests. Some of their feed, such as maize, we should eat ourselves. Halving your meat intake can take down your carbon footprint by 40%.

- Take fewer flights, or none at all. If you must take a holiday, how about a 'stay-cation'? Although it might help to reduce you carbon footprint vastly, this is a tricky lifestyle change in a society in which travel is barely even talked about as anything but an accessible and attractive part of our lifestyle. There are many parts of the world, including nature reserves and forests, which depend on tourism and will disappear if tourists don't come. Nobody wants that. Perhaps we should resolve to limit our air miles rather than eradicate them?

- Drive slower. Tearing around in your car uses more fuel, you get stressed, stress others and it's more likely you'll kill something, such as a barn owl (see page 89).

- Buy an electric car or hybrid. Don't buy an SUV. Better still, buy a bicycle.
- Turn lights off. Try not to leave lights on when you're aren't in the room, or electronic gadgets on standby. If you perform these small changes in isolation, nothing much happens; but if everybody does them, we can save the world.
- Waste less food. This means less food needs to be grown.
- Make sure your home is insulated well.
- Change your shopping habits. Try to buy locally sourced food and other products, and buy food in season. Consider your clothing, a wasteful trade responsible for 3% of global CO_2 emissions.
- Buy less stuff that you don't actually need!
- Use energy-efficient lightbulbs.
- Wash your clothes in cold water.
- If all else fails, try to enter into an effective carbon offsetting programme.

JOINING WILDLIFE AND CONSERVATION GROUPS

If you care for the environment, you're not alone. There are dozens of different conservation groups and societies for those interested in wildlife. There are probably too many, to be fair, stretching resources too thin, and if there were fewer, conservation in Britain might be more effective. The local hedgehog and badger groups should perhaps join forces, although there's the danger in this case of one eating the other (see page 17)! However, as somebody who cares for wildlife, you are duty-bound to join them, as many as you can. Better still, you can give money to them and volunteer for them.

Resources

A Rocha International (www.arocha.org)

Amphibian and Reptile Conservation (ARC) (www.arc-trust.org)

Balloons Blow (www.balloonsblow.org)

Barn Owl Trust (www.barnowltrust.org.uk)

Bat Conservation Trust (www.bats.org.uk)

British Hedgehog Preservation Society (www.britishhedgehogs.org.uk)

British Trust for Ornithology (www.bto.org)

Buglife (www.buglife.org.uk)

Bumblebee Conservation Trust (www.bumblebeeconservation.org)

Butterfly Conservation (https://butterfly-conservation.org)

Earthworm Society of Britain (www.earthwormsoc.org.uk)

Froglife (www.froglife.org)

Game and Wildlife Conservation Trust (www.gwct.org.uk)

Guerilla Gardening (www.guerrillagardening.org)

International Union for the Conservation of Nature (IUCN) (www.iucn.org)

Keep Britain Tidy (www.keepbritaintidy.org)

Mammal Society (www.mammal.org.uk)

Marine Conservation Society (www.mcsuk.org)

MARINElife (www.marine-life.org.uk)

Moorland Association (www.moorlandassociation.org)

National Trust (www.nationaltrust.org.uk)

National Trust for Scotland (www.nts.org.uk)

Nightingale Nights (http://nightingalenights.org.uk)

Operation Turtle Dove (https://operationturtledove.org)

People's Trust for Endangered Species (PTES) (https://ptes.org)

Plantlife (www.plantlife.org.uk)

Red Squirrels United (www.redsquirrelsunited.org.uk)

Rewilding Britain (www.rewildingbritain.org.uk)

Rivers Trust (www.theriverstrust.org)

Royal Horticultural Society (RHS) (www.rhs.org.uk)

Royal Society for the Prevention of Cruelty to Animals (RSPCA) (www.rspca.org.uk)

Royal Society for the Protection of Birds (RSPB) (www.rspb.org.uk)

Saving Wildcats (https://savingwildcats.org.uk)

Scottish Natural Heritage (www.nature.scot)

Scottish Wildcat Action (www.scottishwildcataction.org)

Seahorse Trust (www.theseahorsetrust.org)

Shark Trust (www.sharktrust.org)

Surfers Against Sewage (www.sas.org.uk)

Swift Conservation (https://swift-conservation.org)

Tree Council (https://treecouncil.org.uk)

Wildfowl and Wetlands Trust (www.wwt.org.uk)

Wildlife Trusts (www.wildlifetrusts.org)

Wildwood Trust (https://wildwoodtrust.org)

Woodland Trust (www.woodlandtrust.org.uk)

Zoological Society of London (www.zsl.org)

Acknowledgements

I am most grateful to HarperCollins Publishers for the opportunity to write this labour of love. In particular I am grateful to my commissioning editor, Lydia Good, and my very patient and conscientious editor, Harriet Dobson. Huge thanks, too, to Sarah Edmonds for her wonderfully lively and colourful illustrations that add so much to the book. Andy Lester did a fantastic job of checking through the emphasis and details of the vast complexities of conservation matters.

Love and thanks to my wonderful family, who have to tolerate my extremely occasional fits of writer's grumpiness – my wife Carolyn and my children, Emmie and Sam.